Europe's Rebirth by Tim Buck
First Prism Key Press Edition 2011

Prism Key Press
New York, NY 10001
PrismKeyPress.com

ISBN-13: 978-1466347670

Europe's Rebirth

Tim Buck

CONTENTS

1. Cross Section of World Change

In December 1946 I was elected to attend a conference of representatives of the Communist Parties of the British Empire to be held in London, England, at the end of February 1947. Learning that the Communist Party of Great Britain would be holding its 19th Convention during the same month I arranged to arrive in Britain early enough to attend it also.

My experiences during that trip impressed me deeply. The changes in Britain since I was last there are striking-- particularly in the political consciousness and temper of the people.

I was surprised at the large number of Canadians who have settled in the British Isles since the war. It is impossible to list the names of the dozens of comrades who contacted me, but from the day after I landed until two days before I went aboard ship for my return to Canada I was in receipt of personal visits, calls or letters from comrades whom I have known in Canada but who are now active in the movement in the old country.

During the convention of the British Communist Party I met representatives of Labor movements and governments from literally every corner of Europe[1]. While the convention in general emphasized the profound changes which are taking place in the British Isles, the speeches of the fraternal delegates from the Continent brought a new and revealing picture of developments in the New Democracies. The striking information, and even more the new spirit that they expressed, emphasized the fact that the old Europe of the 1930's, with its evils, is gone; and the popular strength and confidence which found reflection in their speeches testified that it can never be restored.

It became evident that we in Canada need more first

hand information about the radical changes taking place in Europe and the means by which they are being brought about. I decided to visit some of the New Democracies. My selection of France, Czechoslovakia and Yugoslavia as the countries to be visited was determined in the main by the exigencies of the time, travelling facilities, especially the time required to secure visas, permits from the military control to cross the occupied territories, and the need to visit those countries from which I could get a balanced picture of the different types and stages of the developing New Democracy which is spreading across the Continent.[2]

Britain, France, Czechoslovakia and Yugoslavia are the four countries which, combined, illustrate all the stages of development and all the main problems of Europe' New Democracies. In Britain and France the protagonists of the policies and relationships such as led up to the second world war are still strong and hoping to stage a comeback. In Czechoslovakia there is no public advocacy of a revision of prewar policies and relationships, and the country is the most advanced in all Europe towards complete economic recovery. But, and here is a significant feature of Czechoslovakia's politics, interests which want prewar relationships restored are still strong. Their inability to regain their previous dominant influence has reflected in a striking way the "coming together," as it were, of national and democratic popular interests during the war--the growing recognition that today the fight for national freedom and the fight for social progress are inseparable facets of democracy! Yugoslavia, with its infections and stimulation national enthusiasm despite the awful devastation wrought by the war, provides the most vivid and complete illustration of the profoundly revolutionary character of the war of peoples' liberation. Yugoslavia illustrates, also, the relationship between the aims of Europe's New Democracies and the economic prospect of Canada. Thus, while this booklet is not a full description of the conditions in all parts of Europe it does describe the main changes, the purposeful aims and the main problems, which characterize all the New Democracies.

We Canadians, every one of us, will have to concern ourselves increasingly with the developments in Britain and the Empire and in the New Democracies, because those developments are going to change the world during the next decade. In addition there is the fact that nearly all of us have, either directly by birth or indirectly by ancestry, ties of sentiment with the British Isles, France, or with the countries of Central, Eastern, or Southeastern Europe.

The lesson I learned from what I saw in Britain and Europe was that we can have "One World" provided we can arouse democratic people to defend the rights of other peoples to change the part of the world in which they live. When we recognize that we recognize also that the best way to help Canada is to help the peoples of the New Democracies make good the awful devastation of the war, because as Marshal Tito pointed out to me in Belgrade, a well fed, prosperous and economically advancing Europe is an indispensable element for lasting world peace.

Notes

1. I have dealt with the lessons of the Empire Conference separately. "The British Empire in the Post-War World," National Affairs Monthly, April and June 1947.

2. I was also able to make a short visit to Hungary. Because of the distinctive character of the developments in that country, they will be dealt with in a separate pamphlet.

2. Britain at the End of an Era

When the Queen Elizabeth docked at Southampton on February 10th Britain was in the grip of the most severe winter known for fifty years--and "the coal crisis". The weather was extremely cold for the British Isles, roads and railways were blocked by snow, but the real crisis was in coal production. Britain, the country which for generations exported coal to almost all corners of the earth, was unable to supply her own needs. To the shortage of food ant other necessities there was added a drastic shortage of coal. Electric power and railway services were being curtailed. Workers were being laid off as a result of the shortage of fuel and within two weeks the number thus rendered unemployed reached two and a half million. Hundreds of thousands of working class homes were without coal. Supplies to hotels and other public places were curtailed sharply. The government warned the public that "the position of the country is extremely serious"

Britons are "Taking it"

It was cold in the British Isles. Never again will I be able to assure people: "It never gets *very* cold in England." I, along with Bill Foster from the United States, learned differently. Sixteen degrees of frost in London, zero at Oxford and comparable temperatures elsewhere, trains marooned in snow drifts for twelve, twenty, and in one case, at least for forty hours, these and a penetrating "breeze" from the northeast dispelled all doubts. Like when it is cold on the prairie, arguments about the difference between "dry" and "damp" cold seemed irritatingly irrelevant. The London busses are quite unsuitable for cold weather. There is no door at their entrance and not even a pretence of heating them. Taxis are the same and a surprisingly large number of public buildings seemed to be the very centre of the fuel crisis. I addressed a large public meeting in the theatre in the heart of London on February 16th and, because of the fuel crisis, audience and speakers all wore their top coats through the entire meeting. Two of the several families with whom I spent evenings while I was in Britain had no coal when I was there. Bill Foster became an addict to "afternoon tea" within less than a week. "It helps one to get warm" he used to mutter half apologetically as he accepted my daily suggestion. But neither tea nor anything else within our reach could compete with the cold in our bedrooms. Without a speck of heat, no storm windows, and, as the room maid assured me "thoroughly aired every morning," they were frigid. The second night I was in London I put a pair of heavy woollen socks on to go to bed. The third night I wore my shirt inside my pyjamas. After that I surrendered completely and thanked my lucky stars that I had a warm bathrobe with me because after the first few shivering minutes that bathrobe made sleeping a pleasure again. A little more than a week afterward I discovered that Bill, also, discovered the real purpose of a good bathrobe.

Cold weather and shortage of fuel were not the only inconveniences that the people of the British Isles were putting up with. Their housing problem was acute. I learned that nearly eight hundred thousand dwelling units were destroyed or badly damaged in the London area alone by Nazi bombs. Nowhere on the continent, not even in Rotterdam, Holland, did I see anything comparable to the square miles of dest5ruction that one sees in literally every part of London. In the working class districts, particularly around the East India, West India and Surry docks, Battersea, Poplar, Limehouse, Canningtown and Silvertown, there are dozens of areas a quarter to half a mile long and several blocks wide, where not one house remained habitable. Those miles of shattered buildings--in many cases just rubble, are grim evidence of how Britain "took it" during the war and how short Britons must be of homes today.

A hundred times while in the United Kingdom I remarked upon what a good thing it is that the British people have a sense of humor which enables them to enjoy jokes about their troubles. I had dinner and spent the evening with Ben Papworth, who wanted to check up on the impressions he had gained in Canada while attending the .I.L.O. conference as the representative of the British Trade Union Council. "We haven't got much gas for cooking you know, after all, Mr. Churchill needs a lot for other purposes." An elderly and apparently middle class guest was poking the fire in the hotel sitting room in a patient effort to get more warmth. Several of us were watching his efforts with varying hopes when he threw down the poker, straightened himself, and announced: "Well, after all, we aren't going to have to bear so many of the white man's burdens in other countries."

The Source of the Coal Crisis

Exceptionally cold weather and heavy snow, by reducing the amount of coal brought to the surface and impeding transportation was the occasion and immediate cause of the crisis, but cold weather and snow would not have brought a great part of the industrial life of Britain to a standstill except for the deep-seated though less obvious difficulties which had been maturing for a long time. In fact, the coal crisis and its calamitous results did but highlight the situation in Britain's economy as a whole. This fact was made depressingly evident in the "Economic Survey for 1947" presented by the Prime Minister to the British House of Commons while the crisis was at its worst. In a personal Forward to this Survey, the Prime Minister pointed out "Even before the war many of our basic industries were suffering from lack of modernized equipment and there was heavy and persistent unemployment, especially in the development areas.[1] The country failed to take advantage of this surplus labor to bring its industrial undertakings up to date."[2]

The long term factors which were brought to a head by the snow and cold weather were not dealt with fully in the government's survey but they were indicated; along with the suggestion that the Labor Government itself had hitherto failed to grapple with them by repeated emphasis upon the fact that Britain's productive effort in 1946 was limited by weakness in her basic industries. The survey noted that due largely to the lack of mechanization, the average production per worker in the coal mines averaged only 259 tons per man for the entire year. Steel production in 1946 was 12,750,000 ingot tons compared with a pre-war peak of 13 millions and "...the shortage of serviceable rolling stock has seriously curtailed railway capacity throughout the winter. Moreover, the condition of the permanent way and the shortage of timber sleepers (railroad ties) may, in a few months time, make it necessary to impose speed restrictions in the interests of safety. These arrears of maintenance must be made good as soon as possible; otherwise increased production of coal and still will be held up for lack of transport."[3]

The fact that the severe weather had but exposed already existing weaknesses which made a crisis always a probability was summed up in one paragraph in that section of the Survey devoted to a review of economic developments since the election of the Labor Government in 1945.

"The by no means unfavorable industrial results for 1946 were achieved only by a draft of 5 million tons on coal stocks. In a sense, indeed, we have been living on a coal overdraft. The demand for power likewise exceeded the capacity of the power stations; the demand for transport was up to the limit of what could be carried by the railways' depleted rolling stock; the demand for steel was more than could be produced of imported. Indeed our basic industries and services were limiting the nation's productive effort. By the end of 1946 we had reached a stage at which further expansion of our productive effort was vitally necessary, but was extremely difficult unless industry could obtain more coal and power."[4]

The foregoing facts explain how it is that in the active year of 1946 which was remarkably free from interruptions of production, the employed labor force of more than eighteen million people in civilian employment in the highly industrialized United Kingdom produced goods and services to the value of only £7,794,000,000, equal to only thirty-one billion dollars, or about two and a half times the value of the goods and services produced in Canada during the same year.

The relatively low productivity of industry and, therefore, of the national income, is aggravated by the increasing pressure of the cost of Empire upon the common people. The strength of the armed forces at the end of 1946 was 1,427,000, with a further 459,000 employed upon the production of arms, equipment and supplies fir them, making a total of 1,886,000 men and women whose labor power is not available for civilian production and whose activities are financed by taxation. The cost of the armed forces and the activities associated with them under the heading of national defence for 1946 amounted to the staggering total of 1,653 millions of pounds, equal to $6,612,000,000. That is considerably more than a fifth of the value of all the goods and services produced in Britain during the year. The government estimates that its overseas expenditures during 1946, over and above revenue secured by sales of surplus military stores, settlement of war claims, etc., amounted to twelve hundred million dollars.

The cost of trying to maintain the Empire bears heavily upon the masses of the people in the British Isles. It is little wonder that sarcastic comments about the lavish expenditures upon the royal tour in South Africa are frequently heard among all sorts of people.

The sarcasm isn't always obvious. For example, when we arrived in London the papers and the B.B.C. newscasts were generously sprinkled with comments about the Royal Tour. It appears that one of the items that had been emphasized was that the royal family were taking a very large number of towels. I didn't know that and when Bill Foster and I found now towels in our rooms, I sought out the maid: "Can we get some towels in rooms 316 and 317?" I inquired confidently. The elderly maid looked at me without the trace of a smile. "I'm afraid not, sir," she said, "they're all away on the royal tour." She informed me, after she discovered I han't got the joke, that the hotel linen had not yet come back from the laundry but she got us a towel apiece.

The effect of economic weaknesses and other factors noted above is accentuated by the fact that Britain has lost the extremely privileged position that she held in world economy for nearly a century before the war. The government's survey notes that "We have lost gold and foreign investments and have incurred new debts to an extent which implies a worsening of our prewar capital position in relation to the rest of the world by nearly £6,000,000,000.[5] ($24,000,000,000). Along with the loss of overseas investments the United Kingdom has lost the monopoly advantages previously enjoyed in many markets. Her share in the revenue from world shipping and from the financing of world trade are each very much smaller than before the war. The decline of income from overseas is illustrated in a striking manner in the Economic Survey by the figures comparing the balance of payments for the year 1946 with those of the year 1938. Among the figures given, two items emphasize the drastic reduction in the amount of tribute being drawn into the United Kingdom from overseas:

In millions of pounds sterling		
	1938	1946
From interest, profits and dividends (excluding oil, shipping and insurance)	175	60
From other sources (net)	61	10
	236	50

The drastic reduction of income from overseas is only

part of the story. In addition, the United States and Canadian loans and enormous indebtedness to other countries have transformed Britain fro the world's greatest creditor nation to the world's largest debtor nation with the prospect that, if present policies are persisted with in the United Kingdom, the net result of the balance of payments abroad will be an increasing annual drain upon British production instead of supplementing it as heretofore.

It is clear that while severe weather occasioned the crisis in Britain's industry in February, the source of the crisis was in fundamental difficulties of Britain's economy as a whole.

* * * *

Two Fundamental Contradictions

The problem thus created is generally referred to in Britain as the problem of expanding imports sufficiently to pay for essential imports. In its economic survey the government describes it in the following words:

"Imports and exports are of fundamental importance, now and for some years to come. Failure to build up our export trade in the next two or three years so that we can afford to buy enough imports would mean continued food rationing, much less smoking and private motoring, widespread unemployment for lack of raw materials and inability to re-equip industry with the most modern machinery."[6]

On the basis of that estimation of the problem, the government is subordination all other considerations of economic policy in its drive to expand exports and re-exports to 175 per cent of the 1938 total.

It must be emphasized, however, that the Government's *correct* emphasis upon and description of the reason for the vital importance of imports and exports *does not* correctly reflect the fundamental problem of British economy. While it is quite true that Britain must export to pay for essential imports, two crucial questions which the people of the United kingdom will have to answer in the near future are "what is to be the decisive purpose of our foreign trade?" and "what are the essential national financial needs beyond which a struggle to increase exports still further can only increase our economic difficulties?" When those questions are faced frankly and the people of Britain are informed on their implications a revaluation of the aims of Britain's foreign trade and foreign policy will be insisted upon.

The acute problems of the United Kingdom's economy drive, in the main, from two fundamental contradictions. Either of them is sufficient to prevent the solution of Britain's accumulating difficulties within the framework of capitalist economy and each will be deepened by policies now being perused. These contradictions are (a) the contradiction, insoluble under capitalism, between the economic and finincal aims of the United Kingdom and United States finance capitalist monopolies and, (b) the enormous and still growing burden of accumulated claims to unearned increment which weighs like an Alp upon the limited United Kingdom production. It must be emphasized that the claims to unearned increment which bear upon the producers in the United Kingdom have increased tremendously as a result of the war. Capital investment was expanded, largely with governmental assistance, and the accretions of capital continue to reap profits and interest after the war is over. The profits reported by the British industrial and commercial enterprises for 1946 were no less than twenty per cent. higher than in 1943 and £1,150,000,000 ($4,600,000,000) greater than they were in 1938.

In addition to the very high rate of profit taken from industry and commerce, the burden of rent and interest has been increased also. The billions of dollars worth of securities which were stripped off British overseas investments during the war did not dissolve, they were sold by the government to foreign buyers, their previous holders receiving British government bonds in return. Now, for every dollar by which the total of

British overseas investments was thus reduced the government pays interest out of United Kingdom production instead of the British security holders receiving it from abroad. It is clear therefore that while it absolutely true that "Imports and exports are of fundamental importance," there is a wide gulf between the volume of imports and exports necessary to feed and clothe the people of the United Kingdom and keep their industries supplied, and the volume required, if the enormous accumulations of claims to rent interest and profit and other forms of unearned increment, plus the costly panoply of Empire, are to be maintained.

An era is ending in Britain. The golden stream of tribute from colonial possessions and overseas investments is drying up while the cost to the people of Britain of imperialist domination is increasing. At home the demands for rent interest and profit and the weight of hereditary privilege which have accumulated to enormous proportions to the advantage of a few have become so great that the overburdened industrial machine is unable to produce enough to satisfy their demands and still provide for its own continuous replacement and modernization. Investors seek quick profits in luxury trades or speculation instead of in the over-capitalized and outmoded basic industries. Elaborate indoor tracks for dog racing expand and profit fabulously while steel production tends to decline. People with liquid assets are seeking to get as much capital as possible out of Britain of "safe" investment in the United States of the Dominions.

The Labor Government's effort to expand Britain's traditionally large exports to seventy-five percent more than they were before the war is in fact but an attempt to generate a new period of expansion for British capitalism and thus restore some semblance of health to its weakened organism. But, with all the sacrifice that the working people of the British Isles are willing to make this policy cannot succeed. The deep-seated and chronic problems mirrored in the contradictions described in the paragraph above cannot be solved by the policy of trying to enable British capitalism to compete successfully on the world market with the lavishly financed mass production industries of the United States. To make that policy succeed in existing conditions is beyond the capacity of the workers themselves, however willingly they try. Generations of industrial employment have developed in the British working class a reservoir of craft skill that has no equal anywhere in the world. The workers are industrious and painstaking and individually productive, but they are up against the obstacle of having to produce with a national industrial plant of which too large a part is obsolete and by methods of production which have been left behind in other countries, while an impossibly large proportion of their product accrues to that small but powerful group described by the biblical quotation: "They toil not, neither do they spin, yet Solomon in all his glory was not arrayed like one of these."

The only means by which the real national interests of Britain can be protected in this situation is by policies which express frank recognition of the fact that the sacred interests of the people who constitute the nation are superior to the so-called sanctity of the property rights of imperial accumulations of capital. To solve the chronic problems of Britain's national economy in the interests of the great mass of her people requires policies and measures which will strike at their very source. That means to encroach upon the basis and foundations of finance-capital monopoly, of absentee landlordism, yes, of the principle upon which capitalist exploitation itself is founded.

The Contradictions within the Labor Party

The Labor Government as at present constituted rejects the idea of measures which will strike at the foundations of capitalism, Instead, it chooses the policy of buttressing the general structure of British capitalism by state action while finance-capitalist interests are assured by its representatives that, even if all its plans are implemented , "eighty per cent. of British industry will remain under private ownership." It is striving to maintain as much as possible of the old imperialist power and its colonial monopoly by becoming a junior partner of United States imperialism. In the United Nations Organization it stands consistently with United States imperialism against the new Democracies and the U.S.S.R.

It is because of the contrast between the aspirations of the millions who voted for the Labor Party in July 1945 and the policies the government is pursuing that revolt is simmering in the ranks of the Parliamentary Labor Party and among the government's supporters throughout the country.

How widespread this dissatisfaction is, was emphasized to me by a personal experience. Taking a weekend off to visit my native bailiwick in East Anglia I visited my closest boyhood chum, Bert Alexander, in Bungay, Suffolk. Bert had been an ardent supporter of the Labor Party throughout the past twenty-seven years. He has contested elections as a Labor Party candidate. He had scarcely finished shaking hands and introducing me to his wife before he launched upon a serious and extremely well informed criticism of the basic orientation of the Labor Government. His opinion is that placing its dependence upon increasing co-operation with United States finance-capital, the Labor Government may succeed in protecting the interests of British investors but only at the expense of British workers. "What's the use," he asked, "of working our heads off and foregoing necessary wage increases if the only result of success will be to strengthen the capitalist interests, which we thought were going to be abolished, at the expense of the workers who we thought were going to have all the advantages under the Labor Government." Bert's attitude is not at all unusual, even in Bungay.

To appreciate its significance one must understand the political environment in which it develops and how slowly things change there. There is no local branch of the Communist Party in Bungay or in the neighbourhood. The most marked change that has taken place there during the fifty years since

Bert and I played together of "Castle Hills" is the crumbling of the ruins of Sir Roger Bigod's Norman castle as a result of the miniature quakes caused by Nazi bombs. While changing trains at Beccles, my birthplace, I went to the station entrance to take a peep at Station Road. "Are you getting off here, sir?" asked the ticket collector. "No,", I said, " I'm going to Bungay. I just wanted to look up Station Road. You know, I lived here forty-five years ago." "Go on sir," urged the ticket collector, "have a good look. I don't think you'll see any change."

The ticket collector was right. Unless there is more moss on the garden walls there is no change at all in the physical environment. But changing conditions are compelling changes in people's points of view. As Palme Dutt, a fellow East Anglian, explained to me when I expressed amazement at the relatively large number of East Anglian delegates at the Communist Party Congress (they almost equalled the delegation from Wales): "After all, East Anglia produced Oliver Cromwell, projects like that of the Mayflower, men like Tom Paine, as well as Nelson and so on. All those only reflected the impact upon East Anglia of changes taking place in Britain as a whole. Is it any wonder that now East Anglia is producing Communists! Come to our next Party congress and you'll see twice as many."

A political struggle is developing around a series of issues which, in their totality, express the fundamental question of the general political direction and aims of British policy.

The more obvious of the issues around which the struggle is developing within the Labor Party art those relating to foreign policy, the use of the armed forces, conscription, and so on. These are the concrete issues upon which an important and growing body of Labor Party opinion opposes the straining and squandering of Britain's diminishing resources in prosecution of the Tories' imperialist foreign policy. It is no accident that on these issues the government's most solid and enthusiastic support comes from the Conservative Party (even to the extent that Mr. Churchill felt justified in uttering a virtuous protest when the government made a belated concession to Labor opinion in its conscription Bill). The reason for that is deeper and more inclusive than Mr. Churchill's enthusiasm for his own reactionary foreign policy. The source of the different approaches to the problems of foreign policy and the armed forces is to be found in the conflicting concepts of what should be the overall determining aim of the Labor Government's policies--domestic and foreign. As R. P. Dutt has pointed out in a penetrating review of this developing struggle: "In the modern world there can be no separation of home and foreign issues. The fight that is now opening is a fight to save Britain: to end a course which is strangling recovery; to carry the economic and political future of Britain, for the employment and standards of the people, for the lives of men and women and the young generation which is growing up."[7] As Harry Pollit had emphasized, this issue will have to be fought out within the Labor Party.

The Government is aiming to re-establish the United Kingdom as a successful major factor in world capitalism.[8] In pursuit of that aim it is trying to make the United Kingdom valuable to the United States imperialists as an outpost against the New Democracies and Communism on the Continent of Europe. These aims and policies involve acceptance and increasing dependence upon the United States and the salvaging, instead of the abolition, of British capitalism. The Labor Party rebels, as they are termed, reflect, in different ways and in varying degrees, the pressure of working-class opinion which wants to make inroads upon Capitalist profit and hereditary privilege at home and to co-operate with and aid the New Democracies and the U.S.S.R. abroad--a policy which would strengthen the forces making for the abolition of imperialism and capitalist exploitation.

This basic difference is expressed in the conflicting attitudes towards a whole series of concrete questions. Consider, for example, the question of Nationalization. There are different types of nationalization and industries may be nationalized for entirely different reasons. Nationalization which brings all the key industries and financial institutions under public ownership and the control of a government representing the actual producers by hand and brain makes it possible for the government to operate the national economy in the basis of an overall plan--to determine the aims and level of the decisive branches of the national economy and compel the privately owned sectors of the national economy to conform to the national interests. The majority of British workers want this type of nationalization. Their attitude is expressed by Harry Pollitt, when he explains why the Communist Party of Great Britain supports nationalization:

"We know that nationalization under present conditions is not yet Socialism. It does not yet end class divisions and the drawing of rent, interest and profit by the exploiting class. This basic change has still to be achieved. The value of nationalization of a series of key industries in the present reconstruction program lies in the extent to which it serves as a lever to carry through economic planning in the interests of the people to weaken monopoly capitalism and strengthen the working-class movement. We fight for the nationalization of the key industries because it is the only way in which we can secure a planned and systematic organization of work, the rapid re-equipment and modernization of these industries and the increased production necessary to carry through the national economic plan."[9]

There is a different type of nationalization, however, typified in Canada by the manner in which the public treasury was utilized to protect the interests of the investors and speculators, yes, and to line the pockets of the promoters, when a group of railway systems were on the verge of complete physical breakdown as well as financial bankruptcy in 1917. At enormous cost to the Canadian people these broken down--in some cases uncompleted--systems were salvaged and re-organized into one efficient system, the C.N.R., which is an indispensable part of Canada's (capitalist) productive system.

The essential features of this type of nationalization are (a) governmental guarantee of a continued flow of unearned income to those who held the securities of undertakings which, for whatever reason, are not likely to provide them with continued unearned income under private ownership and (b) provision of large amounts of money from the public treasury to make good the physical deterioration which had occurred under private ownership and restore the properties to the level of efficiency necessary for them to be effective parts of the national economy. Clearly this type of nationalization is not Socialism. In fact, the very treatment of such industries as public enterprises, using governmental expenditures to make good deficiencies created by the financial banditry of profit-hungry capitalism, may for a short time strengthen capitalist economy by buttressing it at its weakest points. At best it represents and attempt to reform capitalism: its political essence today and the fallacy of describing it as Socialism is still described correctly in the following, written as a footnote by Frederick Engels seventy years ago:

"Recently, however, since Bismark state ownership, a certain spurious socialism has made its appearance--here and there even degenerating into a kind of flunkeyism--which declares that *all* taking over by the State, even the Bismarkian kind, is in itself socialistic. If, however, the taking over of the tobacco trade by the state was socialistic, Napoleon and Metternich would rank among the founders of socialism. If the Belgian state, for quite ordinary political and financial reasons, constructed its own main railway lines; if Bismarck, without any economic compulsion, took over the main railway lines in Prussia, simply in order to be better able to organize them and use them for war, to train the railway officials as the government's voting cattle, and especially to secure a new source of revenue independent of parliamentary votes--such actions were in no sense socialist measures, whether direct or indirect, conscious or unconscious. Otherwise the Royal Maritime Company, the Royal Porcelain Manufacture, and even the regimental tailors in the army, would be socialist institutions."[10]

A new factor must be noted, however. In whatever nationalization measures have been carried through by the British Labor Government there is one vitally important element which distinguishes them from the type of nationalization described gy Engels in the paragraph quoted above. That element is the role being played by the British labor movement in the fight for nationalization. The role of the labor movement may yet compel the extension of nationalization to all key industries, a change in its character to make of it a means of reducing the amount of unearned income to be produced for idlers instead of a means of guaranteeing its volume, to win full participation by the workers in the planning and direction of industry, and the co-ordination of all key industries within the general framework of an overall national economic plan. These things can be accomplished if the bourgeois ideology and political concepts which are now dominant within the Labor Government are defeated.

It must be said, however, that until now the Labor Government's attitude and policy toward nationalization is one of attempting to reform and modernize Britain's national economy without changing its capitalist character or reducing by a penny the enormous burden of rent interest and profit upon the working class. As noted above, the senior representative of the Labor Government in North America is emphasizing the fact that the government plans to leave eighty percent. of British industry under private capitalist ownership. This is not the policy that the workers voted for when they elected the Labor Government in 1945. They voted among other things for nationalization of industry, rapid encroachments upon the vested interests if finance capital and early amelioration of the burdens now bearing down upon the masses of the people. There is a growing demand now that the government go ahead with the program upon which it was elected. Harry Pollitt voices the sentiments of millions of British workers when he points out: "Production targets will be most easily achieved where the industry is state owned. The government should, therefore, speed up nationalization so that electricity, gas, steel and transport become a strong, planned sector from which the rest of the national economy can be increasingly controlled."[11]

The government's failure to nationalize the key industries and co-ordinate their productive operations is accompanied, as is to be expected, by failure to organize and lead the battle for production in a decisive and planned way. In its survey, the government "justifies" this failure by arguing that such organization would be "totalitarianism". In view of the fact that the government prohibits by law any miner under the age of fifty from leaving the coal mining industry, decides what foodstuffs shall come on the market and the prices at which they shall be sold, orders train services cut, orders electrical power off and on a national scale, and determines which enterprises shall be considered essential and therefore allowed use of electricity, about the only people who treat the argument of "totalitarianism" as though the government were serious in using it, are the Tories. The government betrays consciousness of that fact by adding an assertion that it is impossible to organize and direct the national economy anyway. "Indeed the task of directing by democratic methods an economic system as large and complex as ours is far beyond the power of any governmental machine working by itself no matter how efficient it may be."[12]

With the government adopting such an attitude it is not surprising that there is misunderstanding concerning the battle for increased production in some sections of the trade union movement also. As Harry Pollitt has pointed out: "This is understandable when the workers see pools of unemployment already in former depressed areas, when they read of Cripps talking about the danger of 'coming a real cropper in a year or two...when they see the glaring contrasts between the lives of the rich and the poor, when the troops are called out to break a legitimate strike against intolerable conditions...All the same, our movement must understand that if we do not use our existing productive possibilities to their limit, we have to face the possibility that many of our hard-won conditions and social gains may be placed in jeopardy.'" And Pollitt adds the exact idea which is lacking in the government statement:"We fight for the collective organization of the productive man-power, technical and scientific resources of the nation, so that an all-round increase in every place of productivity can be obtained."[13]

The difference between Harry Pollitt's proposals for the Battle of Production and the government's evasion reflects exactly their different attitudes to finance-capital. Harry Pollitt wants to put the Battle for Production first; the government refuses to do that because it would involve an encroachment upon the freedom of the capitalists to decide what they will produce and how. The government's refusal to encroach upon the basic privileges of finance-capitalist monopoly is reflected even more vividly in the contradictions between what many workers had expected and what they got, in terms of governmental attitude towards workers' demands for improved wages and conditions and increased union participation in the direction of industry. Government spokesmen warn the workers against asking for higher wages. During the road transport dispute the government started out by refusing to put pressure upon the employers on the ground that it could not "interfere in wage adjustment machinery," but shortly afterward, as the strike spread and became stubborn, it found no difficulty in using troops to break the strike.

In the matter of increased labor participation in the direction of industry, the attitude of the government has been expressed in the spirit of Sir Stafford Cripps' declaration that the workers are not capable of managing industry. That statement typifies the government's legalistic, corporation lawyer's attitude towards the entire question. Sir Stanford Cripps, like the majority of members of the government, thinks of the management of industry in terms of the conditions in which the big prizes of management of to the men most skilled in the subtleties of corporation law, or stock market manipulation, or salesmanship--rarely to men whose gifts and training make the problems of production their main interest and concern. This is so because, under the conditions created by finance-capitalism, production is not the main problem in the control of industry. In present capitalist conditions any man or group who can secure a dominant position in relation to legal, stock market or sales problems, can secure and maintain control of a corporation or a group of corporations almost without knowing what they produce, let alone how best to produce it. As Sir Herbert Holt protested when he was able to tell the Royal Commission investigating the textile industry whether or when one of "his" companies produced printed cotton. "That is a matter for operative management."

But the workers of Great Britain voted for the Labor Government of which Sir Stafford Cripps is part because they want to abolish the conditions in which production is subordinated to stock market jobbery, financial manipulation and the vagaries of the capitalist market. They want to establish conditions in which the two determinants of productive activity will be the needs of society and their capacity to produce. In such conditions it will be seen that in the British Isles equally as in other countries it will be free from the ranks of the working class the dependable and effective supervisory and managerial forces will come.

Labor will solve Britain's Problems

The fact there is sharpening conflict between the desires and aspirations of the workers and the policies being pursued by the Labor Government does not mean that the Attlee government is a "bad government." On the contrary, it does but emphasize what tremendous political advance its election marked. Judged in the light of traditional bourgeois governmental policies or by comparison with the Tory opposition led by Mr. Churchill the Labor Government is very advanced. Necessary criticism of its failure to adopt genuine socialist policies must not be misconstrued as suggesting that there is no difference between it and the Tory opposition.

The most advanced workers in Britain, who criticized the Labor Government most sharply for its failure to take its stand definitely on the side of the socialist sector of the world, are the ones who support it most strongly against the Tory opposition. The advanced section of the British Labor Movement criticize the domination of the Labor Government by men who measure policies and statesmanship by standards similar in all essentials to the standards used by Winston Churchill. They want those members of the government who stand blatantly for the maintenance of capitalism and the Empire replaced by men who will fight for working class policies. But the advanced sections of the British working class movement are not going to allow the Tories to exploit Labor Government weaknesses. This fact is stressed over and over again by Harry Pollitt particularly with his systematic insistence that the issue of the main line of governmental policy, domestic and foreign, must be fought out *within the Labor Movement.* The Tories, who at first hoped ghoulishly that they would reap a political advantage from that struggle are learning that this does not mean more power for them as they had anticipated, but the opposite.

This was particularly evident during the coal crisis. The Labor government was not by any means blameless for the very difficult situation which existed. The serious danger of exactly such a situation had been emphasized repeatedly by the Communist Party and by the miners' leaders. As early as June 1946, Arthur Horner, national secretary of the Miners' Union had warned the government and the British people that stockpiles were being depleted and that, unless the necessary measures were taken promptly, interruption of supply by severe weather of any other cause during the winter months would cause a crisis in the national economy and throw a million workers out of employment. The government refused to adopt

30

the necessary measures, however. Instead of taking the labor movement into its confidence it gambled upon the hope for a mild winter and no interruption of supply. To "justify" that decision to drift, cabinet ministers ridiculed the warnings of the Communist Party and the miners' leaders as scare mongering.

Because of that background of the crisis the Labor government was very much on the defensive when the crisis broke. The Tories seized upon what looked like a golden opportunity and launched a violent campaign against the government with the undisguised aim of bringing about either its downfall of a government reorganization--the possibility of a coalition government was mentioned freely. The attitude of the government and the official organ of the labor Party, The Daily Herald, was one of retreat. The Herald actually started to prepare Labor opinion for some measure of governmental reorganization.

That trend was reversed by the militant action of important sections of the trade union movement. Arthur Horner, the miners' national secretary, spoke to the nation over the radio on the issues of the coal crisis and scotched the Tory scheme. Without minimizing the government's responsibility and the urgent need for decisive measures which the government had hitherto refused to adopt, Arthur Horner placed the leadership of the Miners' Union squarely behind the government and pledged an all-out effort by the miners to beat the crisis. The National Committee of the communist Party, through the Daily Worker, gave prompt and vigorous support to Arthur Horner's appeal. Hundreds of union bodies took up the issue--including scores of factory meetings of workers laid off because of the coal shortage. Every one of them without exception rebuffed the Tories and the idea of either a coalition with the Tories or a governmental reorganization to satisfy them. The unions voted solidly to stand behind the government and its minister of fuel and power and administer a defeat to the Tories while beating the coal crisis. Braced by the militancy of the workers, who responded so readily and well to correct leadership. The Labor

Government overcame the tendency to retreat and the Tory offensive was completely defeated.

It is a very significant fact that the section of the British union movement which thus played a decisive role in stopping the retreat by rallying the people behind the government is the section which supports the so-called "Rebels" in the House of Commons and supports the Communist Party's application for affiliation to the Labor Party. The high degree of political consciousness and the deep-rooted class unity illustrated by this is the guarantee that the British Labor movement will find, and unite upon, the path and the policies which lead to the socialist reorganization of Britain's economy at home and fraternal co-operation with other nations which are building Socialism. These workers recognize that now, at the end of the era of world Empire and monopoly maintained by domination, the people of Britain are confronted by inexorable alternatives. Either the policies of the government must be drastically changed to speed up the economic and social reorganization of the country, break the power of finance-capitalist monopolies, build up a planned economy, establish close economic co-operation with the New Democracies, the Soviet Union and the advancing colonial peoples, or Britain will sink to dependence upon the United States, be engulfed in the economic crisis of which the United States is going to be the centre and become enmeshed in the plans of United States imperialism as its advanced outpost in preparations for war against the advancing people's democracy in Europe.

In its own way, and by methods which have become as firmly established as the unions themselves, the British Labor movement is fighting to determine which of these alternatives it shall fight for. The aspirations and deepest hopes of the majority of the British peoples correspond entirely with the perspective stated firs un the foregoing paragraph; but many and severe struggles will have to be fought out within the Labor movement to achieve effective political and organizational unity in the struggle in the struggle to achieve it. There are influential leaders in the trade union movement and influential intellectuals in the Labor Party who will fight against the adoption of such policies by all means within their reach because their own political outlook is essentially bourgeois. They want to limit the role of the Trade Unions and the labor Party to that of opposition to the Tories in a bourgeois state and a capitalist economy. They accept, in some cases without admitting it, Winston Churchill's perspective of the United Kingdom becoming a junior and dependent partner of United States imperialism.

Harry Pollitt breathes confidence that the resistance of such elements will be overcome. In the name of the Communist Party of Great Britain he declares: "...We place our full confidence in the working class, which realizes more and more the decisive role it has to play, both in solving its own problems and the problems of the world. It has the power to change the policy and composition of the Labor Government and force it to choose the right path for the British people."[14]

The magnificent response of the British workers in the first major crisis that they have been called upon to meet since they elected the Labor government testifies that Harry Pollitt is right. The great majority of workers want Socialism in the British Isles and Britain on the side of Socialism throughout the world. They will fight for that aim with ever-increasing strength as issues become clear.

Notes

1. Previously termed the Depressed Areas.

2. Economic Survey for 1947--page 3.

3. Economic Survey for 1947--page 23.

4. Economic Survey for 1947--page 16.

5. Economic Survey for 1947--page 11.

6. Economic Survey for 1947--page 17.

7. "The New Battle for Britain." Labor Monthly, January, 1947, page 5.

8. This aim is implicit in every phase of its economic plan for 1947 expressed in statements such as the following: "But these export targets will not be achieved readily, and in some cases it will be impossible to meet them without a reduction in the amount of production available for the home market."--page 18

9. "Britain's Problems Can Be Solved." Harry Pollitt. Report to the 19th Congress C.P.G.B.-- page 17.

10. "Anti-Duhring."

11. "Britain's Problems Can Be Solved." Harry Pollitt. Report to the 19th Congress C.P.G.B.-- page 12.

12. Economic Survey for 1947--page 8.

13. "Britain's Problems Can Be Solved." Harry Pollitt. Report to the 19th Congress C.P.G.B.-- page 18.

14. "Britain's Problems Can Be Solved." Harry Pollitt. Report to the 19th Congress C.P.G.B.-- page 6.

3. National Rebirth in France

There are striking similarities between the situations in Britain and France, but there are significant and very influential differences also. The similarities derive from and reflect, in the main, the fact that in France as in Britain, finance-capitalist interests and their political representatives still exert powerful influence in opposition to the surging pressure of the masses for democratic progress. The differences may be illustrated by the fact that whereas the United Kingdom one is impressed by the signs that an era is ending; the situation in France is dominated by the intense political struggle to determine the main lines and the perspectives of the era which the majority of French people recognize is beginning. Corresponding with that fact the change in class relationships is more advanced in France--as are the political issues of the day.

The reason for the more advanced stage of political activity in France is to be found in the terrific experiences of its people during the war. France was occupied by Hitler' armies and the armies and police of his collaborators. Under Nazi protection Marshal Petain and his fascist associates tried to make France an active satellite of the Hitlerite axis. With honorable but rare exceptions the French bankers, industrialists, political representatives of big business, generals, admirals, and "men of state", revealed themselves to their stunned countrymen as enemies of their country and its people. They welcomed Hitler's conquest in the hope that he would preserve finance capitalist power and inherited privileges by crushing the democratic movement.

Against the Nazi invaders the best and most devoted sons of France joined hands in united struggle for national liberation. Their anti-Nazi struggle was, of necessity, simultaneously a struggle against Petain's Vichy government and the profiteering collaboration whom it represented. The fight against internal reaction was an indispensable part of the struggle for democratic victory.

Thus, when France was liberated, a large and previously very influential section of the representatives and champions of political reaction had eliminated themselves from French democracy by taking their stand on the side of Hitler and Fascism. In many cases the powerful economic and financial interests which had provided the source and economic basis of fascist pro-Hitler reaction in France were nationalized--several of them without compensation.

In the course of the liberation struggle the democratic forces of the country became more united than ever before. The Communists wrote the record of their devotion to France in imperishable letters of blood. Seventy-five thousand members of the Party were murdered by the Nazis and the Vichy regime-- it became known as "the Party of the executed ones." As a result of the same profound national crisis which exposed most of the pre-war leaders of reaction and rallied the best of the nation under left-wing leadership. French democracy has made a tremendous leap forward. This leap is expressed not only in the new constitution but in the economic and social rights which have been established--including the right of workers in an enterprise to elect their own representatives to participate in its management. Marked progress has been made in the nationalization of industry. The coal mines, gas and electrical power production, aircraft manufacture, sections of the manufacturing industry, the banks of deposit and big insurance companies have been nationalized; and the trade union movement, grown to a membership of more than six millions united in one national Confederation, plays a new and influential role in shaping of national policy. Incidentally. I had the extreme joy of learning that Comrade Fredo Costes, the Secretary of the Metal Workers Federation, who captivated all who met him here in Canada in 1937, was not murdered in a concentration camp as we were previously informed. On the contrary, he escaped and resumed his active participation in the democratic movement. He is again in the leadership of the Metal Qorkers' Federation. In the national elections he was elected again to a seat in the National Assembly.

The central, I think the decisive, immediate problem in France is that of production. The average level of production in French industry when I was there in March was approximately 90% of the average for 1938. Production is some industries, e.g., coal, rubber, rayon, was better than a hundred per cent. of the 1938 figure but in others it was considerably below even the average of ninety per cent. Furthermore, in some industries the problem of restoring production to pre-war levels involves a tremendous amount of construction to make good the devastation wrought during the war. But, as Benoit Franchon, Secretary General of the Confederation of Labor pointed out to me, "It would be a serious mistake to refer everything to the figures for 1938 and adjudge it good or bad accordingly." As an example he explained the problem of coal. The problem or increasing production in general is very largely a problem of increasing the supply of coal to French industry. As a result of extraordinary efforts on the part of the miners, coal production has been increased to 110% of the 1938 figure in spite of the fact that tens of thousands of coal miners have returned to their native lands, particularly to Poland. But increased production in the French mines cannot make up for the lack of coal which was previously imported. Before the war France had to import about twenty million tons of coal per year--largely from Germany. Today France needs more than twenty million tons per year, because, in contrast to the policy of national nihilism that finance-capital with its fear of the democratic trend was pursuing, France must now increase iron and steel production sufficiently to cover all her needs. Benoit Franchon pointed out that this means increasing steel production from a little more than six million tons peer year (the 1939 figure) to fifteen million tons per year. Comrade Franchon summarized the general problem of the national production in the following words:

"We must direct the economic reconstruction of our country, and its modernization, towards an industrial system more complete and more coherent than that which existed forme5rly. It must be a system which insures our economic independence and at the same time permits us to take a ;larger share in international trade."

Is the aim described by Franchon a practical one in the existing situation in France? Jacques Duclos, organization secretary of the nation's largest political party[1] -- upon whose features I noted striking evidence of the intense strain of his historic six years of underground leadership of the anti-Nazi struggle in France--says that it is, and he quotes voluminous facts concerning the resources of France to support his opinion. What he emphasizes above all is the possibility of raising the general level of productivity in France by: (a) correcting the serious weakness in the country's heavy industry--the production of means of production; (b) wider and more efficient utilization of water power resources and building central power and industrial plants close to the mines; (c) raising the technical and productive level of both industry and agriculture by modernization of equipment and methods of operation.[2]

Jacques Duclos emphasizes that these things will be accomplished only if the inexhaustible reservoir of energy and initiative which made the tremendous achievements of the Resistance Movement possible is now evoked in a united national struggle to raise production and living standards to new high levels. That immediately brings forward one of the most acute problems of the battle to increase production; namely the problem of wages and living standards of the working people. The working people of France are not getting enough. The workers, who through their organizations provide the main, indeed the decisive support fir the government's effort to stabilize the franc and prices, are the hardest hit victims of the wholesale evasions of government regulations. Thus, while the franc exchanges for dollars at rates varying from 250 to 350 francs per dollar and prices are up to fantastic levels, workers' wages lag far behind. The average for manual workers, including skilled workers was only forty-five to sixty francs per hour when I was there in March.[3] Expressing the cost of living in 1938 as 100, the cost-of-living index had almost reached 900 in middle of March while, measured on the same basis, wages stood at only 500. Obviously such a situation cannot continue indefinitely and, as Benoit Franchon warned me, the nation's productive effort, and the accompanying battle to stabilize the franc and prices, may be endangered as a result of the greed of manufacturers and speculators who are selling France short in an orgy of black market and other forms of anti-national profiteering.

The Communist Party, which received more votes and elected more candidates than any other party,[4] has proposed a series of measures to stop the orgy of black marketeering, speculation, and the smuggling of real values out of the country. Its proposals include:

a) governmental control of all foreign trade;
b) enforce control of foreign exchange with severe penalties for evasion;
c) enforce price *control* in place of the present "regulation";

d) reform of state finances: all ordinary expenditures to be covered by ordinary revenue, the so-called "dpecial accounts" of the Ministry of Finance to be integrated in the ordinary annual budget and subjected to the scrutiny and control of Parliament, tax reform, correct the present bad relationship of short and long term financial obligations of the government;
e) extend nationalization to investment banks and bank specializing in foreign exchange and re-discount;
f) prompt and drastic action against the black marketeers and against illicit speculation in currency;
g) development of a new relationship of fraternal co-operation with the presently colonial peoples of the Empire;

h) re-establishment of Franc's traditional relationship of trade and friendship with the nations of central and eastern Europe, support democratic forces in all countries, support the principle of big three unanimity in U.N.O.

The above summarizes the main features of the carefully worked out measures which the communist Party proposes as the means by which to assert the interests of the nation against the profiteering interests of speculators and the national nihilism of finance-capital. These measures are part of the comprehensive "Program of Governmental Action" put forward by the communist members of the National Assembly. This program outlines the nation's needs and its immediate possibilities with the rational planned use of available resources in all spheres of the national economy. Manufacturing, coal, electricity, chemicals, petroleum, agriculture, consumers' goods, commerce, prices, currency, foreign trade, reparations, trade agreements and government finances, are each considered as integral and indispensable branches of the country' and properly related targets are proposed for each of them. As Maurice Thorez emphasizes: the prime idea of the program is "organize the productive effort to assure the economic rebirth of the nation without weakening in any way its independence." He adds further that it proposes nothing which exceeds the powers of the National Assembly or the present capacity of the country, while the economic measures propose are the necessary basis for the social advance upon which the hearts of the French people are set.

The reason why such a rational and necessary program is not pressed vigorously as the program of the government is to be found in the transitional relationship of class forces and political parties in France.

The Party which received the largest popular vote [5] and elected the largest number of members to the National Assembly does not head the government. When the result of the voting in the national elections became known a united front of the Right rallied around the M.R.P., drawn together solely for the purpose announced by an official M.R.P. spokesman, who declared that all the actions of the grouping of which it was the centre would be aimed to prevent the establishment of a government headed by a Communist. It was the continuation in a new form of the campaign, previously headed by General De Gaulle, to excluded from governmental responsibility and authority the elected representatives of the most important sections of the French people, the workers and small farmers.

In that situation the Communist deputies in the National Assembly evaluated the interests of French democracy and their responsibilities as follows, as explained by Jacques Duclos;

In the existing situation it is impossible to secure a parliamentary majority in France except through a coalition. It is clear, however, that a coalition government from which the communists were excluded would be a government serving the interests of the trusts and reactionary clericalism against the working class. With such a government there would be serious danger that many of the democratic gains ,made by the people would be swept away. Such a development must be prevented if possible. Furthermore, while the leaders if the M.R.P. had become the centre of a parliamentary grouping dependent upon the extreme Right, many hundreds of thousands among those who voted for the M.R.P. want the democratic program of the Resistance Movement carried through. Thus, the interests of French democracy demanded that the communists participate in the government. The government of democratic union[6] headed by Premier Ramadiet was the result of that decision. In that government the communists, in the interest of national unity, accepted a share of ministries inferior in importance to their electoral strength and their role in the life of the country outside the National Assembly, while the main key posts--Prime Minister, Foreign Minister, Interior, etc.--were held by representatives of parties whose electoral strength and national influence was inferior to that of the Communist Party.

The finance-capitalist interests and elements if clerical reaction, which remain strong, and are encouraged by the attitude and policies of the Untied States government, are seeking now to capitalize on their success in preventing the formation of a government headed by a Communist. Manipulation of prices, speculation in currency and provocative anti-labor agitation is more aggressive than ever. There is renewed and increasingly aggressive pressure for an orientation in foreign policy which would make France dependent upon United States imperialism instead of a leading power among the new democracies of Europe. In their effort to develop a political counter-offensive the reactionaries are now proposing that industrial properties confiscated form collaborators should be returned to their former owners or their capitalist representatives. In the atmosphere created by this organized provocative hostility of powerful finance-capitalist interests to the declared aims of the government and the majority of the electors, the black market flourishes--in currency as well as in goods.[7] Large financial and commercial interests are selling France short in their efforts to get dollar values out of the country.

As Comrade J. Berlioz, member of the National Assembly, pointed out to us, much of the present difficulty would have been prevented if the Socialists had not rejected proposals for electoral unity. The Communist Party proposed a joint Socialist Communist election campaign to unite all progressive forces in the effort to elect a clear parliamentary majority expressing socialist will of the democratic masses. The leaders of the Socialist party rejected the proposal noisily "making eyes" meantime at the anti-communist supporters of the M.R.P. In elections the Socialist Party did not win votes from among the supporters of the M.R.P., in fact the opposite happened, but the combined Communist-Socialist vote equalled 46% of all votes cast and there is every reason to believe that a joint Communist-Socialist slate and a united campaign would have been supported by an over-all majority of the electors.

After the election the Socialists still failed to draw the correct conclusions from the popular vote and could not unite to vote unanimously for a communist to head the government. The result was a closely drawn balance between Left and Right in the government with resulting encouragements to all the reactionary elements in the nation. Such was the situation in which the leaders of the Socialist Party chose again to be "anti-communist" instead of pro-working class and headed the movement to oust the communist ministers form the government.

In France as in Britain the regrouping of political forces is still in progress. The aim of the progressives is to unite all the genuinely democratic republican elements in a united parliamentary force committed to the carrying through of the democratic national and social aims proclaimed by the Resistance Movement. The nation cannot remain for long artificially divided into groupings, each almost equal, one of which wants to continue forward, the other to go back. The democratic aspirations or the French people, expressed with growing strength throughout the past three years, is a guarantee of progressive gains if democracy is allowed free play. The danger is that the very certainty of growing popular support for progressive democratic measures will be seized upon by reaction as a reason for attempts at political adventures aimed to frustrate the democratic aspirations of the people.[8] In the existing relationships such adventurers might endanger the Fourth Republic itself unless they are decisively defeated.

The one means by which to prevent development of such adventurous attempts to destroy the new political influence of the working class is to isolate the reactionary forces and expose them as a tiny minority seeking to betray the interests of the nation. It is evident that, to achieve such a unification of progressive forces and prevent the development of attempts at reactionary adventures in the meantime, will require inspired and consistent work to arouse ever wider masses of the people of France to the recognition of the decisive issues and national needs. It will be a hard and complex task, it may even be a long one, but the French Communists are supremely confident. Maurice Thorez expressed their confidence to us when he said: "We have always believed that the people of France, rich in a glorious tradition, will find their way to more and more democracy, progress and social justice. The task of the Communist Party is to aid, unify and guide them in their struggle."

That is the philosophy of working class leadership which has made the Communist Party the greatest party in France. It is the philosophy of action which guarantees that the forces of progress will be victorious and France will resume her rightful historic place in the front rank of the world's New Democracies.

Notes

1. The French Communist Party

2. In 1938 the average income per person gainfully employed in France was only half the average for those gainfully employed in Britain and only two-seventh the average for all those gainfully employed in the United States.

3. Even at the "official" rate of exchange at the time it equalled only from forty to fifty-four cents per hour. Prices were higher than in Canada.

4. The French C.P. has a million and a quarter dues paying members. It publishes thirteen daily papers in different parts of the country, two of the papers have circulations in excess of half a million each per day. In addition the Party publishes seventy weekly journals devoted to different districts and topics. A majority of all the elected officers of the trade union movement are communists.

5. The popular votes received by the three main parties on Nov 10, 1946, were as follows:

	Vote Received	% of Total Vote Cast
Communist Party	5,475,955	28.2
Socialist Party	3,454,080	17.9
Mouvement Republicain Populaire	5,033,430	26.0
All other parties and groupings	5,198,396	27.9

6. The parties forming the government used this term to define the coalition as one in which the participating parties were each free to propagate their respective programs while maintaining governmental unity.

7. I, along with Comrade Foster of the United States, was solicited repeatedly on the street, in hotel lobbies and on railway stations, to buy Francs at prices varying from 200 Francs to the Dollar up to 275. (The official rate was 112). When we explained that we were opposed to such operations, the people who had approached us expressed amazement. "But this is how everybody does it," one of them said to me.

8. When I was in France during march, there was already wide spread gossip that Heneral DeGaulle's reaction to the failure to exclude Communists from the government would be an attempt to place himself at the head of a new reactionary party aiming at the abolition of the party system.

4. The People's Will in Czechoslovakia

Prague is not so bomb-battered as London--where 800,000 homes were destroyed in addition to the thousands of office buildings, warehouses and factories. At first glance Prague seems to have suffered little if any more than the central parts of Paris. But a short walk in any direction from Wenceslas Square brings a visitor to that impressive evidence of war, the obvious and evident marks of street fighting. I saw it within half an hour of my arrival, first on Stalinova street where it is intersected by Smetanova street. The buildings are heavily pock-marked with rifle and machine-gun fire, with holes to testify that the odd shell found its mark. In walks around the city during the next few days I saw plenty of similar evidence of the fighting which took place in the streets and squares of Prague when the people of the City, led by the National Council of the underground resistance movement, rose against the Germans in May, 1945. The old tow hall, a treasure of Gothic architecture in the main square of the old city, was completely shattered by Nazi shells and gutted by fire. In various parts of the city bomb damage, the marks of shell fire and signs of street fighting all merge in combined testimony.

But, although it is not yet two years since the Nazi soldiers were driven out of Czechoslovakia, the people of this country, under the leadership of their National Front government, have worked so unitedly that the economy of the country is already close to pre-war levels and life is normal in its towns and villages. Of all the countries in Europe this is unquestionably the one furthest advanced to solution of the acute economic problems left as a heritage of the war. Perhaps the best testimony to that fact was the large number of tourists already here in spite of the fact that spring was still around the weatherman's corner. Tourists were to be seen clustered around guides or in couples taking snapshots all over the beautiful, historic and picturesque city of Prague. In the old city square I listened to the story of the noble statue to Johann Huss, who proclaimed in Bohemia the liberal principles first enunciated by John Wycliffe in England, by "standing in" with a group of fourteen tourists who were on a conducted tour . Speaking to one of them for a few minutes, I learned that they were all Americans, Most of them had come on from Paris. Four of them, on the advice of a tourist agency in New York had travelled by air direct from New York to Prague. He informed me confidentially that he and his wife were planning to spend most of their vacation "at the spa in Karlsbad where the kings of England used to take cure."

The appearance of normalcy was heightened by the people and the shop windows. There was little sign of the very expensive luxury goods, particularly clothing, which is still the main feature of ship windows in the exclusive shopping district of London; but the shop windows were well stocked with ordinary clothing, shoes, electric utensils, etc. Prices marked on goods in the windows were considerably lower than the prices for similar types of goods in London. For example, 150 Czech Crowns for an electric iron is equivalent to $3.06. The people were well and warmly clad and shod and, while the rationing of certain foods is very strict, the meals in restaurants were substantial and varied.

Czechoslovakia's annual Trade Fair was held from March 15th to 22nd. As early as March 10th buyers were arriving from places as far apart as Egypt and other eastern Mediterranean countries, France, Belgium, Great Britain and the United States. Czechoslovakia is back in the world market. As I learned during a week if intense activity, the people and government would prefer to devote a great deal more of their increasing production to a rapid increase in their own standard of living and they would do that if they could get credits from countries such as Canada and the United States. But they absolutely must make good the destruction of war.

For example, sixty per cent of their giant Skoda works at Pilsen was destroyed. Its destruction makes a story and an illustration of the attitude of the "Western Allies," in itself. When the Red Army was approaching Pilsen, with the Nazi forces completely demoralized the Skoda plant bereft of raw materials, three weeks before the Nazis surrendered at Berlin, the United States Air Force which had not bothered to bomb the Skoda plant when bombing it might have helped the Red Army, bombed it so lavishly and systematically that only forty per cent. of it was left workable. Nobody in Czechoslovakia will express any opinion as to *why* the U.S. military commanders did things that way but their invariable answer, "We ill build it again," speaks volumes.

Their confidence in the future is striking. Both in Bohemia and Slovakia I found supreme confidence that the government's two year plan, the "Gottwald Plan" as most of the people there term it, will be achieved and surpassed before the end of 1948. This confidence is in fact the measure of the national unity of the people of Czechoslovakia around their government. Because of that as well as the unique features in the political and economic development in Czechoslovakia today, the composition and policy of the Gottwald Government under the presidency of Edward Benes is worthy of careful study by every Canadian who hopes for the continued democratic advance of mankind to socialism.

National Freedom Depends on the People

In August 1944, the Slovak people rose in revolt against the Nazi occupation, starting at Banska Bystrica. The Czechoslovakian Army formations fighting with the Red Army were immediately concentrated in the direction of Slovakia and were fighting on the soil of their homeland by the early fall of 1944. In January, 1945, the Soviet government invited President Benes and his government to establish governmental headquarters in the liberated area of Czechoslovakia. The government proceeded to Moscow from London during march of that year and in April the government, meeting for the first time since 1939 on its native soil, announced its post-war program from Kosice in Slovakia.

The government was composed of representatives of the six Czech and Slovak political parties which has waged war against fascism. The names of the parties are as follows: the Czech Communist party, the Czech Social Democratic Party, the Czech Popular Party (Catholic democrats), the Czech National Socialist Party, the Slovak Communist Party and the Slovak Democratic party (Catholic democrats). These are the six political parties of Czechoslovakia and they are all allied in the National Front based on the post-war program agreed upon and announced at Kosice in April, 1945.

The Prime minister of the provisional government set up at Kosice was Zdenek Ferlinger, leader of the Czech Social Democratic party, who had been the Czechoslovakian ambassador to the Soviet Union. The thunderous events in Europe, the virtual obliteration of the old order of things, first by Hitler and then again by the revolutionary wave which swept the Nazis out of eastern Europe, made it obvious that fundamental changes would have to be made.

The Munich betrayal and six years later under hitler's regime had destroyed most if not all the illusions born at Versailles as well as a lot of prejudices. Throughout those six years the Nazis had tried systematically to destroy the best of the people. Every sign of resistance or of attempt to encourage resistance was dealt with by studied brutality. millions of democratic men and women, who before the war had rejected the idea of united action with the Communist Party because they continued to hope against realities that "somehow or other, the national interest would prevail." learned by bitter and protracted enslavement that the banks, big industrialists and landlords conceive of "the national interest" entirely and solely in terms of their own control of the country's economy and their profit therefrom. These elements accepted Hitler's overlordship without difficulty. Honest democrats learned that only the people will or can be consistent guardians of the real interests of the nation. That is why all democrats in Czechoslovakia applauded President Benes when, emphasizing the inseparable relationship between what happened in 1939 and post-war needs, he declared:

It was already clear to me then that the new war would result in a parting of the ways in modern society and produce a society of universal outlook, consistently democratic and juster in the social and economic sphere than the old. Today we enter upon this parting of the ways, upon new and great changes, upon conflicts concerning it, upon revolutionary processes moderate and conciliant on the one hand, upon revolutionary changes marked by fighting, changes that are local and partial as well as all-European and world changes on the other hand.

It is in the spirit of this epoch of revolution that we must solve all the problems that face us in the sphere of our home policy; and in fact our policy since the 4th of April, 1945--has been pursued in this sense. *In a word, we are reconstructing our State.*"[1]

Czechoslovakia's Two-Year Plan

The Kosice program was formulated in much the spirit of the words of President Benes quoted above. Thus, when the Communist Party received the largest number of votes in the National Elections of May 26, 1946, President Benes called upon Klementi Gottwald to form a new government. It opened a new stage of political and economic development in Czechoslovakia, but did not entail any break in the basic political line and program agreed upon at Kosice. Klementi Gottwald promptly formed a government with representation of each of the parties in the National Front, i.e., all six parties of Czechoslovakia. (It should be noted that there is no official parliamentary opposition.) The *Two Year Plan* which the Communist Party had fought for, and for which its supporters at the polls voted, thus has become the immediate program of the government.

The main targets of the two-year plan are the following:

a) To reach and surpass pre-war production level, by means of large-scale expansion of basic capital and the capital goods production industries, modernization of industry, transport and agriculture, and more effective use of the nation's man power.
b) To mechanize and modernize agriculture. To electrify the countryside, to correct the present unequal distribution of land and the present chaotic division of even small farms into scattered small plots.
c) To carry through tax reform.
d) To complete the currency reform.
e) To simplify and lower the cost of distribution of goods.
f) To industrialize Slovakia.
g) To build up a unified national insurance system.
h) To raise the people's living standards with the increase of production, to lower prices with increased efficiency.
i) To complete the re-settlement of the border regions.
j) To raise the standard of housing by a nation-wide governmental housing program.

As Prime Minister Gottwald ha pointed out, this program is a further development and implementation of the general aims proclaimed by the united democratic parties of the national Resistance at their conference at Kosice in Slovakia during the war. All the parties in the government are pledged to it. The actual targets established for each industry and each sector of the national economy are such that, when it is completed, over-all national production will be 10% above the highest level attained before the war. Then will come all the tremendous advance of Socialist development that the highly developed industry and technique of Czechoslovakia made possible.

The technical and engineering method used in working out the detailed targets of the two year plan bear a striking resemblance to the methods used in Canada during the war. For example: the railways will require 35,000 new freight cars and 1,000 new locomotives by the end of 1948 if all industries reach their target. Inquiries of the steel and fabricating industries and locomotive building plants brought reports showing such a number of freight cars and locomotives can be built before the end of 1948--provided that certain very definite supplies of coal, ore, other supplies and labor are available. Thus the requirements of steel, locomotive and freight car plants for this particular target established and the task of co-ordinating activities in different sectors of the national economy is reduced to exact magnitudes.

Efficient planning has been made possible in Czechoslovakia by nationalization of all the decisive branches of industry and all the decisive financial institutions. Eighty per cent. of all the heavy industry of the country is now nationalized, including 100% of the mines and railways. Light industry is seventy per cent. nationalized. The banks and insurance companies are all nationalized.

The industry of the country is in 17 directorates, each headed by a General Director, two or more Deputy Directors and a central management board. One third of the management board are appointed on the basis of the proposals of the trade unions, the other two thirds must be qualified experts. Such General Directors are now in charge of mining, engineering industries, electric power development, the lumber industry, chemical industry, the glass industry, ceramics industry and building materials, paper mills and cellulose production, textile, footwear, foundries, brewing and yeast production, flour milling, distilleries, the food industry, chocolate and candy production.

Each nationalized plant or establishment is headed by an appointed manager and a "Managing Board." The manager and the members of the board are appointed by the organs of the Ministry of Industry but one third of the members of the managing board consists of elected representatives of the workers employed in the establishment.

The nationalized industry is being organized and operated with the aim of eventual nationalization and economic co-ordination of the entire industry of the country. Just how strongly the workers are behind their government in this is illustrated by the fact that the only strikes that have taken place in Czechoslovakia recently have been strikes in protests against turning plants back to private ownership. I saw one example of such activity. Under pressure the owner of a small factory had sold his factory to a German firm at the beginning of the war. Recently he put in a claim for its restoration to him. Not being in a category specifically designated for nationalization it was returned to him by the government. The minute the workers in the factory learned of it they struck work in a body. They sent deputations to the Cabinet and to their own Central Council of Trade Unions. "The man had been paid for his factory by the Germans. If he had not received a fair price let him apply to the government for supplementary compensation. The factory belongs to the people now and the workers want it to stay this way. Indeed, they would leave it and go to work in a nationalized industry if it did not." The workers won.

What are the results of nationalization? The first response to that question is a comparison of the coal situation here and in Great Britain. The Germans literally raped the mines in Czechoslovakia. Tens of thousands of miners were killed, their average age at the beginning of last year was 45, and the Germans left the railways in chaos with a catastrophic shortage of freight cars. The winter in Czechoslovakia was a great deal worse than in Britain but the government told the miners and railway workers the truth, namely, that there was danger of crisis unless the flow of coal were maintained and increased. The result was that not a single factory was shut down even for an hour at any time through the winter.

The achievement of the miners and railway workers in

keeping every enterprise supplied with coal through the period of severe cold and stormy weather which threw 2,500,000 out of employment in Great Britain, typifies the spirit in which the workers, indeed, the overwhelming majority of all the people of Czechoslovakia, approach the problem of production. An outstanding example of the strong sense of responsibility among workers was provided by the street railway workers of Prague immediately after the Germans were driven out. Street cars had been used to build barricades. Power had been shut off by the workers and, later, the wires, and in some cases even the pillars which supported them, had been torn down to use for defence work. In several places the tracks were either torn up or twisted by exploding shells. When President Benes re-entered Prague at the head of the government shortly afterward almost everything stopped while people turned out to welcome their returning President and government. But the street railway workers held a mass meeting the night before and decided that the best welcome they could give their returning President and government was by getting the city's transportation system running. Thus while the shops were closed and the streets and squares were tumultuous with cheering crowds greeting the evidence of their regained national sovereignty, street railway workers stoically stuck to their work--motormen and conductors joining in the collective job of putting tracks and cars into running order.

Solving the Farmers' Problem

Let it not be assumed from the foregoing that everything has been plain and easy sailing in the national rebirth of Czechoslovakia. Any such illusions are rapidly dissipated by even a little study of the problem which confronted the new government in the sphere of agriculture alone. Realization of the magnitude and complexity of this problem came to me in the course of an interview with Julius Duris, Minister if Agriculture in the Gottwald government.

By way of introduction it should be mentioned that the

minister of Agriculture is the youngest member of the government and the man most hated by the reactionary elements in Czechoslovakia because of the efficiency with which he is grappling with the problems of giving the country's land-hungry peasants a direct voice in the shaping of national policy and farms large enough to maintain their families in decency.

Significantly enough, in reply to my suggestion that perhaps he would describe to me the main features of the problem of agricultural reform in Czechoslovakia, the Minister started out by saying; "We in Czechoslovakia can learn a great deal about the development and mechanization of agriculture from countries like Canada." He then outlined to me some of the needs and problems which flow out of the following facts.

The heart of Czechoslovakia's agrarian problem and the crucial question with the peasantry is land. When the national government was re-established after the war, 96% of all the farmers in the country had less than 20 hectares. The combined acreage of all land held by this 96 percent. of the country's farmers constituted only 44 per cent. of the farm lands of the country. In contrast, one per cent. of the "farmers," that is to say the 16,000 landowners whose holdings averaged more than 50 hectares, had 43 per cent of all the land. Some of those holdings were very large; for example, the area of the Schwartzengerg estates totalled more than 40,000 hectares (90,000 acres).

Breaking the general proportions down, the Minister then showed me that even the figure of 96 per cent. was less than 20 hectares fails to illustrate the real acuteness of the problem because, as he pointed out, "If 96 per cent. had each been farming 20 hectares there would not be such an acute problem." But 70 per cent. of all the farmers in Czechoslovakia had holdings of five hectares or less, and the holdings of this seven-tenths of all the farmers totalled only 15 peer cent. of the total of the land. The first Republic proclaimed a land reform but the peasants benefited ;little from it. 650,000 peasants received one hectare each but 2,000 big landowners had a total of 200,000 hectares added to their holdings. Added to the foregoing facts were two others which derived from the traditional conditions of which large landholdings and landless peasants were a part. One of these facts is that, as a result of land-hunger and the difficulty of securing land hitherto, the holdings of a very large proportion of the farmers, even the small ones, are scattered some times a mile or more apart from each other. There are thirty-three million separate parcels of farm land in n the Republic held by one and a half million farmers. Many farmers have to work 20 or more separate tiny pieces of land--thus precluding mechanization or the use of the most modern machinery and equipment. The other fact is that, because of this scattered character of a large proportion of all the holdings, the level of production per hectare--and in proportion to the manpower dependent upon agriculture--was low.

The aim of the Gottwald govenrment's agrarian policy is to correct that state of affairs and, what is more, the Ministry of Agriculture is carrying the government's policy through. Three decisive measures being carried through simultaneously, as the basis of agrarian reforms are the following:

1) The two million hectares of farm land and the one million hectares of forest, previously owned by Germans and their collaborators and landowners who were traitors, are being given to small peasants. This redistribution is practically completed in Bohemia and Moravia. In Slovakia Peasant Committees are taking over the land and redistributing it rapidly but, for reasons which I will explain when I deal with the specifically Slovakian features of agrarian reform, there is still considerable to be done;

2) The results or the so-called "land refrom" under the first Republic are being subjected to a systematic review . Land which was secured by improper methods, as much as it was, will be expropriated entirely. All other grants will be reduced to 50 hectares;

3) Land is to belong only to those who cultivate it ant the maximum to be allowed to any one family is fifty hectares (about 112 acres). Thus absentee landlordism, which has been a curse, be abolished while the security of title and tenure, combined with various state measures for improving and aiding agriculture will provide long term encouragement to farmers to improve their farms and the volume and quality of their products.

Program for Land Reform

The program for land reform in Slovakia is part of the general program for Czechoslovakia as a whole. But this program, as it applies to Slovakia, was proclaimed in August, 1944, during the uprising against the Germans. It has thus been accepted by all the political parties for a longer period that it has been in operation in Bohemia. At the time that it was proclaimed sale of transfer of the title to land between individuals was also prohibited. As noted above, the actual distribution of land has been carried through to the extent of about 90 peer cent. of all lands rendered available by the verdicts of the people's courts. It should be mentioned that any person convicted by the people's courts as a traitor, automatically loses title to land which may have been in his possession.

At the beginning of the trails it was assumed that government organs would carry through the entire process, from the arrest of suspected persons to redivision of lands and the issuance of titles to the new owners. The Slovakian peasants, however, became increasingly impatient at the long delay between the conviction of traitors and the redistribution of their lands, and, as a result, they established their own local committees to take over the job of redistribution. I learned in Bratislava that, as a result of the speedy action of these committees, 528,000 hectares have now been resettled out of the total of 570,000 hectares rendered vacant by the decisions of the courts. The 42,000 hectares not resettled is land concerning which confiscation is being challenged by the commissioner (or plenipotentiary) for agriculture in the Slovak National Council--he, of course is a Slovakian as are all the members of the national Council.[2]

The way the peasants' committees operate is as follows. The plan for redivision of a piece or several pieces of land is worked out and approved by the committee. The plan is then posted up in a public place for eight days. Anybody who has any cause to criticize it, propose amendments, or to object in any way to its being put into operation, must announce such objection or amendment within the eight days, and any announced objection must be dealt with by the committee. After this process is completed, the plan must be approved by the county committee. Along with the plan, there is also posted up a copy of the terms upon which the new settlers will receive possession of the land. Usually they are obligated to pay, over a term of years, an amount equivalent to the average present value or the crop to be anticipated from such land for two years. Land can be owned only by those who cultivate it.

Plenty of difficulties have to be overcome. One type of difficulty is illustrated by the following example. Consider the case of the huge farm which, before the war, was operated as a joint stock corporation under the name "Economica." Recently, an English lawyer put in a claim for possession of this entire estate, plant and equipment, on the ground that he is in possession of all the shares. He offers in evidence as to when he bought them--whether before the proclamation of the law forbidding the sale or transfer of ownership of land--neither does he submit any information as to whom he received the share certificates from; according to him possession if the share certificates is all that is necessary. How much difficulty can be created by foreign law firms putting in such claims may be estimated by the fact that, before the war there were in Slovakia 132 such big agricultural enterprises organized as joint stock corporations.

Another type of obstacle is typified by the complication in connection with the big estate previously owned by the Hungarian Count Papanin. Papanin was an absentee landlord and a nazi collaborator. His land should revert to the people of Slovakia on either count. But, when the farmers' committee starts to plan resettlement of the land, a Slovakian appears upon the scene with his claim, and what purports to be documentary evidence, that the land is his--that he acquired it from Papanin. Such attempts to obstruct the will of the people are being met with all over Czechoslovakia but they will all be overcome-- even the obstructionists who start out with the notion that their claim will be enforced by British law.

Considerable remains to be done, however. There are still 100,000 applicants for land awaiting resettlement, and the work of official survey and issuance of new titles to ownership is far behind the process of resettlement. Throughout Slovakia the opinion was very strong that, once the Tiso trial was finished the purge of traitors will be completed quickly and the land reform in Slovakia will be completed.

Transforming Agriculture

Simultaneously with the three main features of agrarian reform described above, the Ministry of Agriculture is carrying through two other projects by which the agriculture of Czechoslovakia will be transformed from petty agriculture carried on mainly by human labor, to large-scale modern agriculture, utilizing power and the most efficient labor-saving machinery.

Mechanization will be encouraged by two main measures. The government will advance financial assistance to local community co-operative farm machine and equipment stations, and the government will establish state-owned and operated district stations with modern repair shops, spare parts, supplies, etc.

"But," the Minister emphasized pointing to a chart on

60

his office wall, "machinery and equipment alone won't do the job, we must carry through 'commarization'." Commarization, I learned, is the process by which, in place of all his scattered tiny bits of land, the farmer gets one single piece equivalent to them all. This process is carried out in a cooperative way by the entire village--sometimes even larger areas--coming together with a representative of the Ministry of Agriculture and working out ways and means by which all the land in the area can be redivided so that each family gets its acreage in one piece. On paper it looks like an almost insoluble problem. Some of the peasants are farming bits of land that their forefathers secured, literally as the marks of their freedom. Yet, during the year 1946, the farmers of no less than one thousand communities completed "commarization" of their farms. With the valuable experience of 1946, the Minister of Agriculture has now set his Ministry the target of 3,000 communities to be commarized 1947 and for commarization to be completed throughout the whole of Czechoslovakia in three years' time.

What is the secret by which this Communist Minister of Agriculture, who himself is Slovakian, has been able to unite the peasantry so solidly in support of the Gottwald government's advanced and far-reaching policy? It is simply that by dint of unsparing effort which makes him famous as a man who never rests, he draws the peasants themselves, individually and collectively, into the task of formulating government policy and carrying through. For example: drafts of six government bills dealing with agriculture, prepared by his Ministry under his personal direction, were each submitted to the peasants in village meetings before being finalized for submission to Parliament. Thus, they came before the Parliament very largely as the proposals of the peasants themselves. Reaction, and the more or less veiled supporters of landlordism in the ranks of some sections of the National Front, were incensed at this confidence in the masses. According to their propaganda, Duris is encouraging the farmers to *tell* the government instead of the traditional vice-versa. It is precisely because they fear the increasing participation in public affairs by the people that the reactionary elements in Czechoslovakia hate him as much, even, as they hate Gottwald himself.

It should be added that Duris' confidence in truly democratic processes and his encouragement to the farmers to participate directly in the formulation of agrarian reforms, is the counterpart of the fact that, in the National Elections in may, 1946, the Communist Party received more votes in the rural areas than any other party. Before the war the dominant party in the rural areas was the Agrarian Party. It was, in fact, the Party of the big landowners, the banks and big industrialists. Its replacement by the Communist Party is a measure of the change which has come over Czechoslovakia.

In addition to the measures described above, the Gottwald government is introducing a series of measures which will protect farmers against the prices "sicissors" which bedevils farmers in capitalist countries. In addition to special provisions to protect the interests of farmers in matters connected with taxation, the prices to farmers of certain manufactured goods are regulated by government decree to help maintain parity between the prices they receive for their farm products and the prices they pay for manufactured goods.

As part of the process of encouraging the farmers to participate in the shaping of national policy and of helping them to understand how it is that national planning is possible once the big capitalist interests are eliminated, the Ministry of Agriculture has developed a nation-wide educational campaign. Twelve hundred different films have been made, depicting practically every phase of peasant life and of its problems. The films are with sound. While able to understand but a few words of the language spoken, I can vouch for their very high quality in all other respects. Mobile projection sets with generators and sound apparatus take these films into every village. It isn't a gift from other taxpayers. The peasants pay and ask for more, and more and more. Along the same line of action mobile theatres tour the villages. Libraries have been established in six thousand villages where there were no libraries before. On the First of May, 1947, a new stage of the campaign to raise the cultural, political and material standard if life in the villages is to commence. In five hundred villages where there is no such facility, the government will establish several millions of Crowns to send elected delegates representing the farmers on visits to countries with higher standards of agriculture.

A good indication of the thoroughness with which the Gottwald government is developing the new life in the rural communities of Czechoslovakia, is the fact that an attractive pamphlet is being distributed to farmers un tens of thousands of copies by the Ministry of Agriculture, describing Canadian agriculture and the great advantages secured by its efficient technique.

While thanking the minister for the opportunity to make an intensely interesting study of the work of the Ministry of Agriculture, of which I have here only been able to indicate the main outlines, I expressed the wish which, I assured him, is shared by hundreds if thousands, yes, millions of Canadians, that we in Canada could help the farmers of Czechoslovakia a little more than by the example of mechanization. "But you can," he responded warmly, "Canada has seed grain, breeding cattle, tractors, modern farm machinery and agronomic developments among the finest in the world. Czechoslovakia needs more of all of these things. Of some of them, for example seed grain and breeding cattle, we are desperately short. Your country, which has helped Czechoslovakia more than once in the past, could help as tremendously now."

I learned afterward, that the government of Czechoslovakia would like to purchase such things and many others in Canada if only it could get credit which will enable it to do so. Democratic Canadians who welcomed the substantial loans to Britain and France, and who deplored the granting of a credit of $50 millions to the government of Holland to be used specifically in the attempt to crush the Republic of Indonesia, should certainly press the Dominion Government to grant substantial credits to help the people of Czechoslovakia build their new and democratic social order.

National Equality in a Legislative Union

Two nations occupy the lands of Czechoslovakia. In Bohemia and Moravia live the Czech people with a population of approximately eight millions, in Slovakia live the Slovaks with a population of three and a half millions. he Czech people and the Slovak people have each occupied their present lands for many centuries. Throughout the generations when what had been the kingdoms of Bohemia and Slovakia were included as "conquered provinces" in the Austro-Hungarian Empire, and their schools and national institutions suppressed, these peoples each retained their deep and abiding consciousness of nationality and the affinity of their mutual interests as nations.

The depth and strength of the national sentiment among the people of each nation, which has been a powerful factor in their struggles for freedom, sharpened national dissatisfaction in Slovakia during the years between the first and second world war. The Slovaks were dissatisfied with the attitude, all too common in the first Republic, and not entirely absent from the "London government" during the war that the people of Czechoslovakia were one nation--"Czechoslovaks" thereby denying by implication and vital historical fact that they are two nations. Czechs and Slovaks. That attitude alone was bad enough but what the majority of Slovaks objected to even more was what they called the "Czech monopoly" that it reflected. Industrial development was obstructed in Slovakia because the great industries were located in Bohemia and Moravia and their owners, many of them Germans, wanted to maintain their monopoly of the home market. Such industrial development as did take place in Slovakia was largely because the industries and financiers in Bohemia wanted to exploit some natural resource, e.g., lumber or coal, not so abundant or so readily available in the western part of the country. Furthermore, reflecting the general tendency, a large proportion of government employees in Slovakia--too large a proportion in the opinion of the Slovaks--were Czechs. Thus, to the people of Slovakia the political continent of attitude that the people of Czechoslovakia were "one nation" appeared to be a tendency to relegate the Slovaks to an inferior position.

Let me emphasise the fact that the above is not a description of the attitudes of the masses of the people of the two nations towards each other. In fact, the economic factors and the class interests which fostered friction between the two nations were in opposition to the real interests of the Czech people also, and they fought tenaciously against them. Friction between the Czech and Slovak nations was a result of uneven economic and cultural development on the background of centuries of effort by alien rulers to Hungarianize the Slovaks and Germanize the Czechs.

While it would be wrong to exaggerate the effect of those mutual differences, it would be even more wrong to ignore it. Vice-Premier Viliam Siroky, Chairman if the Communist Party of Slovakia, emphasized to me that the exploitation of the friction they caused enabled the fascist Hlynka movement to win support from the tens of thousands of Slovaks. Hitler's so-called protectorate under the traitor, Tiso[3] was in some respects a reflection of the shortcomings of the manner in which the national question was dealt with in the first Republic. Because of these facts, what I am going to write about the solution of the national problem in Czechoslovakia will be mainly about Slovakia. A little consideration will show the reason for this: that is the core of the national problem.

The Gottwald government has proclaimed its intention to prevent any recrudescence of Slovakia's justified dissatisfaction in the first Republic by establishing--and protecting by constitutional guarantees--full national equality for the Slovaks. Furthermore, Gottwald agrees with Vice-Premier Siroky when the latter emphasizes that the Slovaks will not be satisfied with simple administrative equality, they insist upon full and complete political national equality. The Slovakian Communist Party declares that the requisite and guarantee of the unity of Czechoslovakia is the existence of conditions, constitutional and economic, which ensure that the Slovaks shall enjoy complete sovereignty as a nation. In other words, only as equal nations exercising completely equal rights and jointly guaranteeing the unity and sovereignty of Czechoslovakia, can the Czechs and Slovaks solve their peculiar national problem. Gottwald himself emphasized this fundamental point when he stated the position of the communists of Bohemia, Moravia and Slovakia on the national question, in the course of the national conference of the united resistance forces at Kosice during the war.

The Gottwald government is committed to the principle of guaranteeing full national equality to each of the nations of Czechoslovakia. The problem now to be solved is that of fulfilling the aspirations of the two nations--whose languages differ little more than the speech of the Scots and the English, whose economy is even more mutually dependent, and who have so recently shared in two periods of joint struggle for national freedom--without establishing artificial distinctions, which the reactionary elements might seek to make into barriers between them.

The plans now in operation are aimed to guarantee complete national equality and fraternity between Czechs and Slovaks by advance along three main lines:

a) constitutional guarantees;
b) industrialization of Slovakia;
c) elimination of all differences of opportunity between Czechs and Slovaks for cultural, economic or political development.

Let us note the proposals in each of these fields.

The most authoritative declaration on the question of constitutional guarantees was made by Prime Minister Gottwald in his official report to the National Constituent Assembly on the program of his government. Concerning Czech and Slovak relations Premier Gottwald said:

"The new constitution will emphasize that the Republic is a national state of Czechs and Slovaks...in a constitutional guarantee that only the Czech and Slovak nations will in future decide in all public an national affairs...

It is obvious that the new Constitution must embody a new settlement of the relationship between the Czech and Slovak nations. This will be based on the Kosice agreement program, and the experience gained in its application will be taken into account. In any case, the new Constitution must recognize the Slovaks as a separate nation, as expressed by their legislative and executive organs--the Slovak National Council and the Committee of Delegates. Equal rights with the Czech nation, while maintaining the unity of the Czechoslovak Republic, must be ensured to the Slovaks; indeed, this unity must be further strengthened."

In accord with the aim thus indicated, we find Slovaks sharing equal terms with Czechs in all spheres of politics and administration in the central government and simultaneously developing special organs to serve their distinct national needs. One novel result of the new and bold approach to the national problem is the Slovak National Council. This body is a new type of national assembly. Its 100 members are elected by the Slovakian electorate, separately from its election of deputies to the central Parliament of Czechoslovakia. This central Parliament sits in Prague but the Slovak National Council sits in the ancient and beautiful capital of Slovakia, Bratislava on the banks of the Danube.

In passing it should be noted that, as yet, there is no Czech counterpart to the Slovak National Council. The most nearly similar body in Bohemia and Moravia is the Czech national Committee. But, as Vice-President Viliam Siroky and Comrade Bastovansky, General Secretary of the C.P. of Slovakia, each emphasized, this only illustrates the fact that, to a large extent, the new government organs have been developed empirically to meet concrete needs.

The Slovak National council arose as an organ of the national struggle against Hitler. As Comrade Smidke, its vice-chairman, explained to me: "The Slovak National Council was the leading body which united all anti-fascist forces in the national liberation movement. It continues and will continue as an essential organ of national reconstruction and Czechoslovak unity. It will play an important role in the shaping of Czechoslovakia's new constitution."

Vice-Chairman Smidke has good reason to be proud of the Council and its wartime role. He, Smidke, was a member of Parliament before the war. Coming from Prague to Slovakia he remained within the country in a leading role in the Party's struggle against Hitler and his quisling agent Tiso, all through the war. He was the first Chairman of the (illegal) Slovak National Council when it was formed. He became chairman of the general staff of the united resistance forces. When Comrades Siroky and Duris (now respectively Vice-Premier and Minister of Agriculture) were caught by the Gestapo and sentenced to death, Smidke went to Bratislava and directed the audacious coup by which they were enable to escape. When I met him it seemed fitting that he should be at the new headquarters of the National Council--the place which the traitor Tiso used as his residence while he governed Slovakia for Hitler.

Corresponding with the national Council there is a Slovakian governmental organ, the Council of Commissioners or plenipotentiaries (Poverenik). This is a body composed of Slovakian plenipotentiaries representing each department of the central government except Foreign Affairs, Foreign Trade and National Defence.

The Committee (or sub-cabinet) of Slovak Povereniki is

the Slovenska executive for the central government: the central government operates in Slovakia through the Poverenik. For example: in Slovakia the Two Year Plan is carried through under the direction of the Slovak Poverenik for Industry. With the Slovak National Council, elected by secret ballot on the basis of a wide democratic franchise (every citizen, male and female, over the age of 18 has the right to vote), and Slovak sub-cabinet of Povereniki, Czechoslovakia is exploring new possibilities and new methods of achieving complete equality and unity of purpose for two distinct nations in one legislatively unified democratic state.

But, as the leading members of the Communist Party of Slovakia emphasized to me repeatedly while I was in Bratislava and other parts of Slovakia, notably Hlinik and Limbach, constitutional reforms are indispensable but not all-sufficient measures to ensure the national sovereignty and economic equality of the Slovak people. To ensure those two related aims there must be added to the constitutional reforms *industrialization.* Whereas Bohemia became industrialized contemporaneously with and as a part of the spread of capitalist industry, Slovakia must be industrialized now as an essential part of the building of the new society. The need for it, they emphasized, is decisive; and the success of the Two Year Plan will be measured very largely by the extent to which the need is met.

To raise industry in Slovakia to the same average level as it now is in Bohemia requires that it be doubled. Thus, the Two Year Plan aims to get started the major developments which will create more industry in Slovakia during the next four years than was developed during the entire forty-six years of this century. This will be accomplished by:

a) Large scale utilization of Slovakia's resources which are immediately available. These include the building of twelve hydro electric power stations to generate a billion K.W.H., exploitation with modern machinery and equipment of two big coal deposits discovered recently and modernization of the other mines, the establishment of a basic steel industry in Slovakia, extension of the secondary branches of Slovakia's forest products industries, especially wood fabrication and pulp and paper.

b) The transfer of machinery and equipment, largely from the Sudeten area, to Slovakia to double the textile, boot and shoe, rubber and chemical industries.

c) A radical reorganization and improvement of the entire transportation system of Slovakia: electrification of certain key stretches of railway, double-tracking of large stretches with road beds to carry heavier and faster traffic than at present. The River Vah will be made navigable and a canal cut to connect the Danube and Oder Rivers thus giving Czechoslovakia a direct route for freight to the Baltic. surfaced highways will be constructed, at least between the main industrial centres.

d) Because industrial development will attract large numbers of young people from the farms the plan for industrial development of Slovakia includes, also, immediate and long-term measures for aiding Slovak agriculture. At the present time a much larger proportion of the population of Slovakia depends on agriculture than is the case in Bohemia and Moravia, but the Plan proposes to help the farmers overcome this weakness by increased use of fertilizers and machinery, and greatly improved methods of livestock and dairy farming.

e) All the plans for the rapid expansion of industry in Slovakia will depend to a great extent upon the capacity of the building industry. Slovakia is the part of Czechoslovakia that suffered the most material damage during the war. Big battles were fought in the eastern part of the country and an enormous amount of building is required even to make good the devastation of the war. On the other hand the building industry in Slovakia is still, in the main, in the hands of private contractors. This is not entirely because they are small concerns, for forty-five percent of all of them in Slovakia employ 500 workers of more. It cannot be said, either, that it is because they are all loyal to the Republic; but the fact remains that the tremendous tasks of building and construction planned for the next two years depend on an industry which is predominantly in the hands of private owners and contractors and operates very largely upon a small scale and handicraft basis.

As a step towards improving this situation the central government has allotted three hundred million crowns to be expended under the direction of the Slovak Poverenik for Industry; for machinery, equipment and general mechanization in the building industry.

As indicated above. the main immediate emphasis is upon industrial reconstruction development or transfer which will produce quick results in the form of industrial employment and production in Slovakia. But the comprehensive scale upon which the general plan for Slovakia's industrialization is conceived is indicated by the fact that in the two year period of 1947-48, four billion crowns will be spent upon the development in Slovakia of power, steel and chemical industries alone.

The industrial developments planned, with the higher level of productivity and higher living standards that they will bring to Slovakia, will eliminate the economic inferiority which was the basic source of the friction which prevented the development of completely equal and fraternal unity of the two nations in the first Republic. As Viliam Siroky pointed out in a penetrating public lecture on the subject, to which I had the great pleasure of listening: "The coping stone which will tie together the aims and results of constitutional reforms and Slovakian industrialization is the growing consciousness of our nations' joint interest in maintaining and strengthening the unity and economic and political strength of Czechoslovakia." To establish the conditions which will generate and fructify such consciousness is, as Gottwald declared to the Constituent National Assembly, but to "be worthy trustees of the legacy of our dead, and conscientious executors of the mandate of the hiving." It is to carry out the people's will in Czechoslovakia.

What Sort of State is Czechoslovakia?

The question is often asked: "What type of state is Czechoslovakia?" More often than not the questioner finds it hard to accept the answer that "It is a democratic people's state differing in several of its fundamentally progressive features from the traditional capitalist state, but it is not a socialist state."

There is a widespread tendency to assume that the sole reason for saying that it is not yet a socialist state is because it is not based upon Soviets, but that is entirely wrong. Czechoslovakia may become a socialist state without Soviets, indeed, the government and President Benes indicate that they look to such a development. But, if only because the President and the government nave declared their aim to establish "new forms of ownership, *alongside* private ownership and co-operative ownership"[4], it is necessary to emphasize that the People's Republic of Czechoslovakia is not a socialist state because capitalist production and private profit still operate in important sectors of the country's economy and, within the limits defined by the government, are protected by the state.

An important part of the national economy is privately owned and operated for private profit. That is true, also, of the country' agriculture. The grain trade, indeed all the wholesale trade, including both buying and selling is still controlled by private capital and some big reactionary interests are operating in that field. Retail distribution and the fields of commercial activity related to wholesale and retail trade are also operated by private capital. Important elements of the manufacturing industries are still owned by private capital. There are still large landowners, and many who used to own vast estates, share in the rich profits of monopolies or enjoy other class privileges, are still hoping to overturn the present regime and regain the privileges that they used to enjoy. Reflecting the fact that capitalist interests are still entrenched in important sectors of the national economy, the political representatives of capitalist interests are still active and exert an important influence upon the political life of the country. Finance-capital seeks persistently to undermine confidence in the future of the new democracy and to bribe public opinion with illusions about the assurance of generous assistance from the United States if only Czechoslovakia would adopt policies similar to those pursued in Turkey.

There is a persistent, although not noisy, undercurrent of propaganda in favor of what the people who spread it term "a western orientation." Reactionary interests are pinning their hopes upon and turning their support to the popular Party in Bohemia and the Democratic Party in Slovakia. These two parties are each in the government. Each of them holds four seats in the Cabinet. They were each established during the national liberation, expressing mainly the political mobilization of Catholic democrats. Each of them has become a base of operation for political elements whose avowed stock in trade is anti-socialist and anti-Soviet politics. Thus, while all the parties are committed to support the government's program the strength of reactionary interests, and their increasing aggressiveness, is reflected in the markedly different degrees to which the different parties are prepared to fight to carry that program through.

The political life of the country reflects these facts. The struggle to base democracy squarely and irrevocably upon the masses of the people, the struggle to carry through the nationalization decrees consistently so as to make the nationalized sector the decisive sector of the national economy, even the struggle to carry through the land reforms, each has to be carried on against resistance. Sometimes the resistance is open and aggressive, sometimes it takes the form of obstruction, but always it reflects the hope of rallying and organizing opposition to the policies of the government. In this struggle the leadership of the Czech Popular Party and the Slovak Democratic Party represent, in general, the weakened but still strong forces of reaction. Between them and the cooperating Communists and Social Democrats there is the National Socialist Party , which has recently opened its ranks to ex-members of the Agrarian Party (suppressed for collaboration with the Nazis).

The character of a state--or of its economy--can be defined correctly only in terms which correspond with the character of its political authority and the interests that it represents. It is clear, therefore, that it would be inconsistent with political realities to define Czechoslovakia as a socialist state.

It would be equally wrong, however, to ignore or minimize the profound changes that have taken place and are still in progress in Czechoslovakia. Six years of occupation during which the Nazis crushed every sign of resistance with incredible brutality and tried systematically to destroy the elite of the nation dissipated illusions among workers, farmers and city middle-class people. Recognition of present day political realities combines with tradition and widespread Marxist understanding to unite the majority of the people of Czechoslovakia in the desire for and support of policies aimed at the socialist reconstruction of their country. Against this united national will to progressive social and economic change the forces of reaction will fail. Already the state organization in Czechoslovakia and the functions of its government have undergone a radical change. This change is not fortuitous, as is shown by the following words of president Benes to the Provisional National Assembly on Oct. 28th, 1945:

"In the history of the world and of Europe this period will present a special, great chapter swollen with the extreme ferment of revolution: it will be reckoned among the most stormy epochs of world history and will be designated a transition, a break, and a process of creation, at the price of grave crises, wars and human sufferings, of a new phase of human society, or at least human sufferings, of a new phase of human society, or at least as an attempt at the commencement of such creation."

As emphasized by President Benes, the Czechoslovakian state is being reconstructed. As a result of thes carefully planned reconstruction Czechoslovakia is a very advanced democracy. The National Assembly and the government are elected by secret ballot in direct elections on the basis of universal suffrage with complete equality for both sexes, and proportional representation. Each party nominating candidates receives seats in proportion to the vote it receives from the electorate and each party which supports the governmental program is represented un the cabinet also in proportion to its electoral strength. Thus, the 26 members of the Gottwald government are drawn from and represent six parties and each, except the C.P. of which the Prime Minister is a member, is represented by a vice-premier as well as by the members holding its share of the cabinet post.

The advanced character of Czechoslovak democracy is expressed in other ways also. It is provided by law that newspapers and periodicals must be owned by public associations; i.e., trade unions, societies, religions bodies, associations of trades or professional people, etc., political parties, or the state. They cannot be owned and published by private individuals, companies, or anonymous owners. As a result, newspapers in Czechoslovakia are organs of opinion as well as media for the circulation of news, and the press cannot be monopolized or dominated by men of great wealth as is the case in Canada and the United States.

Other expressions of the high level of Czechoslovak democracy will be embodied in the new constitution if it is finalized on the principles outlined by Premier Gottwald. Inasmuch as all six political parties are in the government and have declared their agreement with those principles it is at ;east very probable that the constitution will include the main features that Gottwald indicated, which include the following:

"The new constitution must also embody the great complex of decrees on the nationalization of banking, mines, mineral resources, power and the big key industries...On the other hand, the constitution must give protection to small and medium-sized private enterprise, and especially the legitimately acquired property of our farmers, tradesmen,, shopkeepers, and all other persons and corporations must be safeguarded."

The principle of constitutional provisions that banks, insurance companies, railways, mines and heavy industry shall be owned by the state monopolies, is a very advanced democratic concept which will not be found in the constitution of any state dominated by capitalist interests. As is also the principle that the state must guarantee to its citizens the right to work which Gottwald emphasized as follow:

"The new constitution will express the principle that every citizen has the right to work, to a fair reward for his work, the right to education, recreation, and to maintenance if he is incapable of working...

Finally, the new constitution must guarantee the full equality of women, personal and civil liberties, freedom of religion, freedom of the press, of speech, freedom of assembly and association, freedom of scientific research, freedom of artistic expression as well as all other personal and political freedoms guaranteed by the present constitution. The Judicature will be exercised by independent law-courts."

It is evident, therefore, that Czechoslovakia is a new type pf state. It is different in several fundamental respects from the states dominated by the capitalist class and operating on the basis of bourgeois democracy. Czechoslovakia is a people's democracy. It is a democracy in the service of the great mass of the people; workers, farmers, tradesmen, professional people, and intellectuals. Contrary to the traditional capitalist pretence that the state stands above classes and has no direct function in the productive activities of the nation, the government of Czechoslovakia assumes very definite responsibility for the direction of industry and finance and for guaranteeing, directly and specifically, employment, food, clothing, shelter and education, to every citizen. Assumption of these new functions marks a sharp break with the past and a sharp break with the governmental policies of capitalism.

While private ownership in the means of production and, therefore, production for profit, are still big factors in the national economy and, backed up enthusiastically by the workers, is pressing forward to the socialist organization of the country. The people of Czechoslovakia have their eyes upon the goal of socialism and they will achieve it if peace is maintained.

Notes

1. Presidential message to the first session of the Provisional National Assembly, October 28th, 1945.

2. I will explain below the extremely interesting structure and political and administrative status of the Slovak National Council and the "Povernik"--a sort of Cabinet of Slovakian Plenipotentiaries parallel to the national government.

3. It is significant that the Vatican recognizes that Tiso was tried and convicted for activities outside his role and duties as a priest.

4. President Benes: Address to the Provisional National Assembly, Prague, October, 1945.

5. The People won in Yugoslavia

The Federative People's Republic of Yugoslavia is a product of the war of national liberation, One is impressed by marked differences between Yugoslavia and Czechoslovakia and the differences are almost entirely the result of the different experiences of the two countries during the war. Yugoslavia suffered invasion by Italian and German armies. Italian Fascists and German Nazis wrought terror and devastation upon the people and the country. The destruction of towns, villages, railway structures and rolling stock was enormous.

A million seven hundred thousand of the people of Yugoslavia were killed. I, along with Bill Foster, visited what had been a concentration camp a few miles from Belgrade. In this camp alone 250,000 men and women accused of suspected for membership in or aid to the Partisan movement had been murdered. We were shown the "execution grove" to which the prisoners marked out for destruction were taken each day to be machine-gunned into big open pits dug the day before by other prisoners.

The German troops and their quisling Yugoslav servants indulged in shameful vandalism as well as brutal cruelty. Entire villages were systematically destroyed by shell fire of by flames merely on the charge that men from there were fighting in the partisan forces or that somebody in the village was aiding the partisans. Sometimes entire families were wiped out to make sure of getting one member suspected of being a partisan. Comrade Kovachevich took me up to the Tomb of the Unknown Soldier on Mount Khavala one day; even that had not been immune. The memorial is a dignified and striking work of art, built of hard black granite. At each of the two entrances to the tomb itself there is posted a symbolic guard of honor composed of twelve-foot figures hewn out of the same black granite and beautifully chiselled to represent at the one entrance, Serbia a, Croatia, Montenegro and Slovenia, and at the other entrance, Macedonia, Herzegovina, Bosnia and Dalmatia. They are the work of the famous sculptor Mestrovic. I should mention that a statue of "Mother of Prayer" by the same sculptor stands in the Ontario Art Gallery. The tomb has no possible military value and the fact that it could not have been struck by shells intended for another target is obvious by its remoteness. Its location is beautiful--from it one can see the confluence of the Sava and Danube rivers within which Belgrade is nestled--but that is all. Yet the tomb was shelled mercilessly. Fortunately, none of te figures within the entrances was damaged but the outer walls of the tomb and the wall surrounding the memorial as a whole are severely battered. Repair work was just being started while I was there.

But neither vandalism upon their villages and monuments, not the threat of physical brutality against their persons, daunted the Yugoslav people. The Germans, Italians and their hated Yugoslav quislings destroyed entire families--but other families enrolled to take their place in the partisan armies. In hundreds of villages the entire population enrolled en masses in the partisan armies, sometimes firming a unit named after their own village. These men and women knew no quarter in the war, and they knew no possible end to it except victory, by which they would regain their farms, their rights to live freely as nations and to govern themselves freely as they choose.

I am not exaggerating. In Yugoslavia I was able to see and study the terrible experiences of its people during the war, as well as their post-war hopes and desires, the more intimately because, in addition to the splendid comrades whom I had met before as fellow delegates at conferences of in Spain I had the help, as translators and companions, of Canadians who landed behind the lines on Yugoslavia by parachute during the war. Some of these comrades are continuing their service in struggle for the new democracy. Not all of them: some are back in the working class struggle in Canada; and some, like Comrade Paul Stickman, sleep beneath the warm earth of their native land. Among those who stayed to help build the new Yugoslavia I was lucky to meet Bob Prpich. Bob is married now. Rosa, his charming wife, was an active partisan who by active service won her commission in a combat unit, and is now a full colonel.

Speaking of women in the partisan armies, I should mention that the wife of the Prime Minister of Serbia was one of a family of six girls--all six of whom were in combat units of the partisans. Consider the record of the family of one of our comrades who went from Canada, Nick Kovachevich. He, like Tito and so many other leaders of the Yugoslav workers and peasants had been forced to flee the country to escape Alexander's reactionary police dragnet. His father and mother and other members of his family continued their support of the struggle for freedom. Nick's brother Sava became a leader of the peasants in his locality, guiding them and teaching them throughout the bitter years of monarchist reaction.

When the people of Montenegro started to organize their partisan units to resist the invaders and their quisling tools, the Kovachevich family did their part. Nick's father, despite his age, promptly enrolled with the partisans. Nick's two brothers, his wife (who did not know that Nick himself was training in far-away Canada to parachute into Montenegro) and his two sons, the wife of one of the other brothers, and Nick's daughter who had been a baby when he was compelled to flee the country, were all in combat units of the partisan armies. The mother, Johanna Kovachevich, 75 years old, was left in the village to cultivate the farm and care for all the grandchildren who were too young to fight.

Her youngest son, Sava Kovachevich became known as the Chapayev of Yugoslavia. The name Kovachevich became synonymous with deathless national resistance. Denounced by a quisling and searched out by fascist troops Johanna Kovachevich, then aged 77, was arrested as a hostage and thrown into a concentration camp for partisans along with the babies left in her care. A prominent Yugoslav quisling, upon whom Hitler and the King had each bestowed the title of General, went to her in the camp. In reply to his insinuation that her life and the lives of the children depended upon her denouncing "the devils she had borne," the old lady inspired every imprisoned partisan by declaring bluntly, with simple pride: "You cannot frighten me because the sons I bore are patriots and heroes, their names will be honored throughout Yugoslavia when yours will have become a curse."

When the old lady was eventually set free from the concentration camp, Nick's wife visited her. The old lady looked at her and asked, "Is it true that Sava is dead?" The daughter-in-law nodded silently. "And my husband?" The daughter-in-law nodded again. "Tell me," said Johanna, and the daughter-in-law told her sadly that her husband and Sava, her other son, and one of Nick's sons had all been killed in action. The old lady, then nearing 80 years of age, looked straight in front in silence for a few moments, then lifting her head and looking straight at her daughter-in-law she said simply: "But we are free!" When Comrade Nick Kivachevich introduced me to his heroic mother, I felt both honored and humble. This dignified old peasant lady cannot read of write, but she has never wavered in her devotion to the people's cause and her confidence in their eventual victory under the leadership of the working class: that' she so richly deserves the decoration that she wears--the highest bestowed in Yugoslavia.

By such unmeasured heroism and sacrifice the people of Yugoslavia compelled the Nazi high command to keep three-quarters of a million troops in that country, thereby contributing substantially to military victory. Five major offensives were organized against the Partisans by the Nazi high command in efforts to wipe out organized democratic resistance within the country. Each offensive inflicted new destruction upon the country, new terrors upon the people and a heavy toll of life among the organized partisans, but each failed. The Partisans, hardened and tempered in their struggle against the invaders, emerged from each offensive more deeply rooted among the people. In bitter unyielding struggle the Partisans built up their forces, developed brilliant military leadership, and transformed themselves form scattered bands of guerrilla fighters into national armies and finally into the powerful People's national Liberation Army of Yugoslavia.

The organizing and directing force in the ranks of the partisans and the masses of the people was the Communist Party of Yugoslavia. The Party led the struggle to unite in liberating all democratic freedom-loving people of the nations which constitute the Southern Slavs. In Yugoslavia, as elsewhere, the struggle against Nazi occupation was and had to be simultaneously a struggle ageist the financier, landlords and politicians who collaborated with the representatives of Mussolini and Hitler. In Yugoslavia this part of the liberation struggle was earlier and more openly a large-scale military struggle than in any other part of the occupied countries The line between the people who wanted Yugoslavia to be free and those who were allied or collaborating with reactionary interested in one or other of the great powers was sharp. As Boris Kidrich, Minister of Industrialization, said to me: "Our revolution took place in the course of an implacable struggle against foreign invaders who occupied our country, partly in collaboration with and partly due to the misrule and cowardice of the old ruling classes."

The old ruling classes had been in the service of imperialist interests before the war. The royal family, and the clique of aristocrats, industrialists and bankers most closely associated with it, had been, for decades concerned mainly with amassing personal fortunes by their hangers-on fled the country at the beginning of the war; those who did not flee the country joined the invaders. When the war ended the old ruling classes, from the king downward, had lost not only the power but every pretence of moral right to come back to Yugoslavia and re-establish their criminal misrule. Thus the People's Authority, which had been developed in the liberated areas during the war was over and, through the organs that they had already established the people of Yugoslavia were able to determine freely the immediate fundamental questions of post-war national organization and reconstruction.

Developments and experiences during the war exerted an influence upon the decisions made, It has been imperative to press the effort to reorganize the national economy in the midst of the war. The Peopl's Authorities had developed energetic campaigns to raise production and to stamp out the black market as an essential part of the fight for national freedom. In the process a large part of the national economy has resumed operation under governmental direction and control. It was in fact but the codification of the property relationships and forms of management which were already operating when the elected National Constituent Assembly wrote the following fundamental laws into the constitution:

Chapter 4: Social Economic Organization

Article 15.

"In order to protect the vital interests of the people, to further the people's prosperity and the right use of all economic potentialities and forces, the state and co-operative sectors, while achieving a general control over the private economic sector.

In carrying out the general economic plan and economic control, the state relies on the co-operation of syndicalist organizations of workmen and employees and other organizations of the working people.

Article 18.

Private property and private initiative in economy are guaranteed.

The inheritance of private property is guaranteed. The right of inheritance is regulated by law.

No person is permitted top use the right of private property to the detriment of the people's community.

The existence or private monopolist organizations such as cartels, syndicates, trusts and similar organizations created for the purpose of dictating prices, monopolizing the market and damaging the interests of the national economy is forbidden.

Article 19.

The land belongs to those who cultivate it.

There can be no large land-holdings in private hands on any basis whatsoever."[1]

All mineral and other wealth underground, the waters, including mineral and medicinal waters, the sources of natural power, the means of rail and air transport, the posts, telegraphs, telephones and broadcasting facilities, the industrial undertakings and power plants, the banks and other financial and commercial institutions and trading operations other than retail trade and petty commerce are nationalized and operation of them is directed by the public authorities to serve the needs of the people. Similarly it was a direct continuation of the forms and methods of management and administration which had been developed during the war when the Constituent Assembly decided that management and direction of the nation's economic life must be on the same level as its ownership, i.e., under the control of the People's Authorities: municipal, provincial, national or federal.

In the preparation of legislation which bears directly upon workers' interests, the Central Council of Trade Unions (of the national Council if the legislation is one of the National Parliaments) participates as a body in study of the draft proposals and by officially submitting its own criticisms or amendments.

A new federal system of social security legislation has already been enacted guaranteeing the working people of Yugoslavia complete social security. Operation of the social security machinery is shared in by the organized workers through their own organizations. The law guarantees sex equality in all spheres of economic, educational, cultural or other professional activity, the right to work of maintenance, equal pay for equal work, vacations with pay. Old age pensions are payable at the age of fifty-five. There is no means test. The law provides that married couples who qualify shall each receive the full pension. The Yugoslav trade unions are affiliated with the W.F.T.U. At the conclusion of the three-hour enumeration of such achievements the General Secretary of the National Council of the Untied Trade Unions of Workers and Employees said to me simply: "In general, Comrade Buck, the situation of the working people is very much improved but we need a great deal more yet and we are aiming to improve our situation a further 100 per cent. through the Five Year Plan."

The Five Year Plan

Yugoslavia's Five Year Plan is the first stage of an audacious long-term project for the complete industrialization of that country. It was worked out on the basis of known natural resources and productive capacity.

The general plan for all Yugoslavia combines within itself each of the five year plans worked out to provide for concentrated effort to speed up industrial development in these sections of the country where economic development is particularly weak, with the aim of "leveling up" the degree if industrialization in each of the national republics.

The Minister for Industrialization explained to me some of the special features of the economic basis from which the plan has to start and some of the features which provide big possibilities for development. He pointed out that old Yugoslavia was one of what may be termed the "middle" industrial countries of Europe. Industrially it was a land of contrasts. Rich mineral resources were exploited by foreign capital, in some cases by very modern methods, in others by methods that were almost primitive. Such secondary industries as were developed also revealed marked contrast between modern plants operated largely for absentee owners and others using almost primitive production techniques. Supplemented by certain important additions to machine tool and similar equipment, the existing forces of production, even after the terrible destruction wrought during the war, will be an adequate basis for the industrialization of the country, given the hydro-electrical power development which is one of the primary targets of the plan.

The first Five Year Plan is aimed to expand heavy industry so that Yugoslavia can produce her own means of production. It includes plans for several large undertakings, including the building of a big hydro-electric power plant and an aluminium refinery close to the richest bauxite deposits in Europe.

The targets set in the field of power development and heavy industry are specific and limited. In addition, the plan provides for the tremendous expansion of production of consumers' goods and there the only limit is to be physical capacity.

Each industry works out the details of implementing the plan. Big enterprises have their specific targets already established and socialist competition, between sections of industry, between groups of workers, and between enterprises is in full swing. All such socialist workers or individuals who excel are very substantial. Every increase in production is paid for directly in the proportion that it constitutes advance from the average 1946 base to the target set for December 1951.

Yugoslavia's agriculture has not been collectivized but very far reaching reforms have been carried through. In conformity with the fundamental law written into the Constitution "the land belongs to those who cultivate it," all the great estates have been broken up and the land divided among the peasants. Special governmental measures are in operation to assist poor peasants, particularly those with small of medium-sized farms. For these, credit is available at very low rates of interest and they benefit by substantial tax exemptions.

To help develop efficient methods of cultivation and increased productivity the government has established tractor and implement stations to serve the farmers. Several hundred such stations are already in operation--their number is limited only by the limited possibility of buying tractors and other agricultural machinery from the United States and Canada.

The main channel through which the peasants are drawn into active participation is the campaign to carry through the Five Year Plan in the co-operative movement. Village co-operatives are the organizations through which the peasants, collectively sell their products and buy manufactured of imported goods. Furthermore, to an increasing extent the village co-operatives are taking over the management and operation of the local production, of which there is a great deal in Yugoslavia. Thus, in two hundred and fifty villages already, soap, malt, beer, tanned hides, shoes, and a score or other products to fill the immediate needs of the peasants are produced by the village co-operatives. The People's Authorities are doing everything possible to help that development. In this there is illustrated both the change in the role of the co-operatives in Yugoslavia and the basis for hope that they will become very important features of a new type in the building of socialist society.

In old Yugoslavia the co-ops were, by force of conditions over which they and their members had no control, integral parts of the capitalist economic system, subjected in common with all small businesses to the banks and their finance-capitalist policies. Today, however, the co-operatives are a secondary part of the publicly owned and operated economy in a country in which finance-capitalist monopoly has been abolished. Al branches of banking and finance are now public services, and the predominant character and direction of economic development is determined by the Five Year Plan. In these conditions there is solid ground for the opinion, held by leading members of the government, that the co-operatives can be a very important factor in the building of a socialist society.

The great need of Yugoslavia today is to increase productivity, i.e., reduce the cost of production. The Five Year Plan, with the tremendous advance that it will bring in the technical level of industry and the more efficient utilization of the country's resources, will be a tremendous factor in this increase of productivity as will, also, the socialist competition in which the conscious will of the workers to increase production expresses itself.

The decisive factor in the struggle for increased production is the highly developed political consciousness and idealism of the Yugoslav workers. The People's War of Liberation freed the land or Yugoslavia from the Nazi armies of occupation, it freed the Southern Slavs from hated national inequality and subjection one to another and, the decisive achievement, it freed the people as a whole from the servitude which was previously their lot. The deep popular devotion to those aims was the source of the unwavering mass heroism displayed by the people of Yugoslavia during the war. Pride in wartime achievements, and the mass determination to maintain them, is the source of continuing mass heroism in the popular struggle for economic reconstruction.

The enthusiasm of the workers often expresses itself in unanimous decisions of the employees in industrial enterprises to work overtime--sometimes without pay--in a collective effort to put their enterprise out in front in the national race to the next intermediate target of the Five Year Plan. The extent of this may be realized by the fact that the National Council of Trade Unions had to take up the matter officially and warn against the danger of over-enthusiastic militants among the workers leading them into efforts which might exhaust sections of the workers and bring an unfavorable later reaction.

Yuagoslavia's Five Year Plan is going to succeed. It will be completed before the end of five years. Marshal Tito, who delineated the main political role and objectives of the plan and participated actively in its elaboration is, by his own confidence--which is no less sure when expressed in private conversation--a guarantee that the task is well in hand.

But the people are not going to have to wait until the Five Year Plan is completed before they enjoy some of its fruits. Comrade Kidrich, the Minister for industrialization emphasized this to me again and again. "Remember,", he said to me in the midst of answering a question as to the overall possibilities for the expansion of basic socially owned capital during the next five years, "our first concern is to raise the living standards of our people." Bit, I said, you must build your socialist industry. His reply so impressed me that I got him to repeat it while I copied it word for word as it was translated: "*We are* building a *socialist society.* The nationalized sector of our economy is already socialist in that it is owned by the people, operated under the control and direction of the people's authorities, is dominant in the economy of our country. In the sense of the transfer of power, our socialist revolution has been carried through and the transfer of power has been the more complete because it followed the utter breakdown, cowardly abdication and national treachery of the old ruling class. These latter things we have yet to attain. Our people are solidly united in their determination to achieve an economy of abundance and we must always place the aim of immediate increased popular well-being right in the forefront of all our plans and activites."

The Youth in Socialist Construction in Yugoslavia

A politically alert observer needs to be in Yugoslavia but a short time to recognize that, next to the Soviet Union, this country has made the greatest political strides in the forward march of the new People's Democracy. In no phase of the country's activities is this more evident than in the activities and political role of the youth. *#8220;The People's Youth Movement of Yugoslavia" with its membership of a million and a half young men and women is more than just a very strong organization, it is a vibrant, integral and influential part of the nation's force organized to build the new and democratic life.

A description of the multifarious activities initiated and maintained by the Youth Movement would require more space than is available here. It should be explained, however, that one of the special and justified prides of youth of People's Yugoslavia today is the fact that the ranks of the partisans and later of the People' Army of Yugoslavia were made up mainly of very young people. Between seventy and seventy-five peer cent. of all ranks in the Yugoslav People's Army of National Liberation led by marshal Tito were youth. Most of the generals of Yugoslavia are still young in years although many of them established their reputations as gifted and resourceful military commanders in the gruelling war against fascism in Spain before they became leaders in the war against German and Italian invasion at home. The heroic role that the youth played in the war for national liberation gives the organized youth a high place inn the nation today, particularly in the three spheres in which the People's Youth Movement assumes special responsibilities. These three fields are:

a) Education--from the organization of kindergartens to the campaign to wipe out illiteracy;
b) Cultural activity--from the translation of the classics into the various languages of the national republics of Yugoslavia, to raising the level of the traditional folk arts, the re-creation of truly national theatres, etc.;
c) The role of youth in socialist construction--from the development of local study classes to the actual construction of big national undertakings.

Because this third special responsibility assumed by the Youth Movement embodies elements of the other two, I am going to devote this section to a description of the source and development of the amazing plans for mobilization of youth volunteers for big construction jobs and some of its results.

The tradition of organized voluntary labor became established among the youth during the struggle against the invaders. As early as the spring of 1942 the Young Communist League organized systematic campaigns in which the youth rallied the people and organized them to get production restarted on territory liberated from the fascist occupation troops. A high level of youthful endeavour and leadership was attained even during that year. An area of rich agricultural land was liberated but the Nazi troops remained within a few hundred yards of the partisan lines and shelled the area frequently. The peasants did not believe it was worthwhile even to try to plough and seed the land, so the Y.C.L. organized special brigades of volunteer youth for the job. They gathered together farm tools and equipment and they ploughed and seeded the liberated soil to within a hundred yards of the Germans' trenches. They were shelled, sometimes machine-gunned and once tanks were sent out to disperse them. The cost to the Germans in tanks was such that tanks were not sent a second time. The land was seeded and, such was the importance of food, from that day the determination to hold that land inspired every family and brought new recruits to the partisan ranks. When the crop, an excellent one although a little late, was taken off un the late summer, the idea of voluntary mobilization for essential work was already established as an essential feature of the war for national liberation. In such actions the youth, to the end of 1945, contributed no less than forty million days of voluntary labor to essential tasks such as bridge repair, agriculture, railway, factory and housing repairs.

During a conference in January, 1946, the leadership of the Youth movement, now become "The People's Youth Movement of Yugoslavia," had a point on the agenda which could be translated: "How to mobilize more of the youth for even larger undertakings." Reports of the pledges given by the youth in all parts of the country showed that hundreds of thousands of the youth were inspired by the idea of mobilization for voluntary work and the youth leaders grasped the possibility for a really grand undertaking. There and then the conference adopted the proposal to build a stretch of railway by a large scale mobilization of the youth for voluntary work.

The stretch of railway decided upon was in northeastern Bosnia. It is a district possessed of very rich natural resources. Even while Bosnia was part of the Austro-Hungarian Empire the government of Franz Joseph had announced the plan to build a railroad there but nothing was done. After Versailles the government of Yugoslavia announced again the plan to build the railway but again nothing was done--as one of the comrades remarked to me "apparently the negotiators at the Yugoslav end were holding out for a higher rake-off from foreign capitalists." The conference decided that what an empire and a pro-fascist monarchy had failed to do should be done in one summer by the mobilized youth of the People"s Republic.

A draft plan was prepared in consultation with engineers. On April 12th, 1946, the State Economic Council endorsed the plan and authorized the National Youth Movement to undertake the work. A call was issued to the youth of the nation to mobilize for voluntry wok with a specific and categoric warning that no young worker already employed in industry and no student who was behind in his studies would be accepted. Volunteers had to apply to the headquarters of the youth movement in their locality and, it being an honor to be accepted for this greatest enterprise that the youth had so far undertaken, it was the volunteers who had to prove that they should be accepted.

On May 1st 14,000 young men and women were already at work on the site with tools and equipment for preliminary work and the job was started. Before the end of May, 62,000 youth from all over Yugoslavia were at work building the railway and by the middle of June their numbers were swollen by more than 2,000 volunteers who came from other countries to share this vital experience. One of the comrades describing this interjected at this point that "there was one very good volunteer form Canada."

The youth were organized in brigades. In many cases entire brigades came from a single village. Work was carried on in three shifts and in six months ninety kilometres of roadbed and track were completed. The comrades laughed about the new type of competition which developed. It was a competition between the engineering staff and the construction brigades. Quite early on the job surveyors and engineers had been startled when work which they had estimated would take five days was done in one. From that day forward it was the construction crews pressing the professional engineers instead of vice-versa.

When the work was first started there was a lack of skilled personnel so training courses were established. Right on the job young men and women were trained as bulldozer operators, rockdrill operators, welders, rivetters and so on. Recreation, entertainment, cultural activity and so on was necessary and, as a result, a whole cadre of leaders of a new type for youth centres was developed. Illiterate youths learned to read and write, others learned to be regular railway operators to work on the road after it was finished. Never before to the knowledge of the people in this part of the world had anything of the like ever been accomplished. Some days more than three kilometres of roadbed and track were completed in twenty-four hours. A tunnel was drilled through rock at the speed of six metres per day. Plenty of difficulties were experienced. Two hundred metres of roadbed was washed out around the side of a mountain so it was decided to go through instead of around. It was getting late in the summer, rain increased difficulties, but a special crew of 2,000 finished the tunnel as an additional proof of their capacity and the ninety kilometres of railway was completed within the scheduled six months.

As a result of that great material and moral achievement, for the youth and the whole nation, the People's Youth

Movement is undertaking to build an even bigger piece of railroad this summer. The stretch to be built this summer will be no less than 237 kilometres (about 150 miles) long, also in Bosnia, to tab an area of extremely valuable mineral and forest wealth. It will be a big job. Three and a half million cubic metres of earth have to be moved, eight bridges have to be built, a mile long tunnel has to be cut through rock. Work will start on April 1st and the plan is to complete the railway in seven months. The target for the working forces is 180,000 volunteers. Most of them will come from different parts of Yugoslavia, of course, but the inspiration for the idea guarantees that several thousand will come from other countries. I was amazed to learn that an entire brigade (250 workers) will arrive from Iran before the end of April. I read a letter from Australia explaining that ten young workers were already on their way from that country on the S.S. Asturias. The letter described each of the ten, explained that they had their return tickets and money for expenses which they had saved but that they would need advice as to the best way to travel after landing and giving an address in Paris to which such advice should be sent. Other similar letters are from places as far apart as the Scandinavian countries, South Africa and the United States.

By April first a hundred and fifteen brigades of about 250 workers each will be at work. On this road the work day will be six hours instead of eight. Camps are being built now all along the route and commissariat, maintenance, repair and other centres are being established and equipped in advance. The first job to be accomplished is the construction of a temporary track over which to transport supplies, equipment, etc. Profiting by the rich experience of the last year, special sanitation units, a medical corps and hospital facilities are also in operation in advance of opening up work. In addition to training youth for construction there will be special course to train youth who desire to remain and work on the road after it is completed. One thousand hectares (2,2250 acres) of land in several parcels along the route are already planted with seed for early vegetables, some of which will be ready during April. The railway will have its own athletics division: soccer, basketball, volleyball and organized hikes, its entertainment division: theatres, library and reading rooms and its own newspaper. The editorial and technical staff of "Borba" (The Worker) the official organ of the Communist Party of Yugoslavia has undertaken to organize and publish the daily paper right on the job. Printing machinery is already on the site being readied to start publication on April first. A cause for even greater pride among the youth is that the railway is also to have its own radio which, while helping to entertain and inform the youth working on the road, will give the people of Yugoslavia--and the world-- a "blow by blow" account of the building of the road.

The foregoing describes the plan for just one great enterprise that the organized youth of this country undertakes to complete this summer by collective voluntary labor. There are other projects. In Montenegro another, although much shorter railway will be built. In Belgrade an entire factory building will be built from foundation to roof. In every one of the six republics at least one major undertaking and several local ones will be completed. The brigades for The Youth Railway of 1947 were recruited while I was there. In local youth festivals, which were in progress in preparation for the World Youth Festival at Prague, the ambition to go to work on the railway was even more vocal than the evident enthusiasm about the great gathering of world democratic youth to be held at Prague. Hundreds of thousands of young men and women were announcing their intention of combining a month or more of voluntary work on the Youth Railway with their attendance at the World Festival at Prague. What a wonderful experience, and what an achievement it would be of a brigade of Canadian youth could have participated in this great socialist adventure.

What Type of State is Yugoslavia?

The question frequently asked concerning

Czechoslovakia is also asked about Yugoslavia: "What type of state is it?" The answer is some what different from that given concerning Czechoslovakia in that it must be said unequivocally that the new Yugoslavia is not a capitalist state. While not a Soviet state and not a proletarian dictatorship, the National Front government headed by Marshal Tito is a people's government and Yugoslavia is a people's state in every sense of the word.

It is true, as the Minister for Industrialization emphasized, that the economic and cultural wounds inflicted by the fascist occupation armies will have to be healed and tremendous economic developments will have to be carried through before it can be said that Yugoslavia has a socialist society. But, bearing his warning in mind, it must be said that insofar as internal economic and political organization is concerned, Yugoslavia is definitely started on the task of building Socialism. The property relationships, state forms and social forces within the country are such that she requires only to be granted peace to develop her industry and cultural institutions and she will be a fully socialist society in a short time.

The fact which guarantees such a result if Yugoslavia is granted peace is that the socialist aim of the government expresses the united democratic will of her people. The popular and deeply considered will which was expressed in heroic struggle and torrents of blood during the war has been repeated in elections since.

There are people, particularly editors of capitalist newspapers, who either cannot believe of else refuse to admit that the majority of the people of any country would choose freely to support genuinely socialist policies. Yugoslavia is one of the best illustrations of how completely wrong such people are. Yugoslavia demonstrates in a striking manner how only with such policies can the people maintain their freedom from the servitude and national inequalities against which in a very large measure they were fighting during the war. This patent fact is obvious in several fundamental features of the new constitution. It is particularly obvious in the fact that the several nations which constitute the peoples of South Slavia have fashioned their new state to express and correspond with their equality as nations and their unity as equals in place of the past discredited relationships of national inequality and mutual hatreds.

I had the great pleasure, indeed the privilege of sharing a meal and spending an evening with Marshal Tito and several members of the central committee of the C.P. of Yugoslavia. It was remarkable to meet again the comrades whom one had known previously as delegates at conferences or volunteers in Spain, and to find that they are now members of the government, experienced commanding officers in the National Army, or leaders in the nation's economy. It was even more remarkable to note how unequivocally they placed the government's approach to the national question as the key to the achievement of Socialism. Marshal Tito, whose genius was the guiding and unifying force which personified both the heroism and the aspiration to complete national freedom of all the Southern Slavs, places this as the primary and fundamental factor un the success of the liberation struggle. In his report to the Party Conference held, illegally of course, in Zagreb during the summer of 1940 (the conference at which the Party prepared itself for the great historic job that it did during the six years which followed), Tito emphasized again and again the central issue of the democratic national rights of the nationalities. Writing about this issue recently Titi commented as follows:

"A considerable amount of patient work was needed in order to convince all the nationalities that it was only through the National Liberation struggle, through the struggle against the invaders and the local reactionary forces, that all their national rights could be achieved and a new Yugoslavia thus created...once all the peoples of Yugoslavia had become convinced of the correctness of the policy which the communist

Party of Yugoslavia had laid before the masses, the national question became one of the powerful driving forces in the liberation struggle."[2]

Milovan Djilas, one of the heroes of both the International Brigade in Spain and the liberation war in Yugoslavia, now minister without portfolio in the federal government enquired first about Bill Kardash, then gave Bill Foster and me some very pertinent facts which illustrate both the importance of the national question and the consistency with which the Communist Party fought for a correct solution of it.

The Southern Slavs consist of five distinct nations. They are: Serbs, 6,500,000; Croats, 4,500,000; Slovenes, 1,250,000; Montenegrins, 350,000 Macedonians, 1,300,000. In addition there are national minorities, particularly Albanians, 800,000, Hungarians, 450,000, Germans, 80,000. In the provinces of Bosnia and Herzegovina there are elements of several nationalities, members of no one nation constituting a majority, in addition to which about fifty per cent. of the people are Moslems.

An important difference between old Yugoslavia and Czarist Russia is in connection with the national question that, while among the Southern Slavs national consciousness was more highly developed that was the case with many nationalities in Czarist Russia, the Serbian monarchy and the ruling class which it headed sought continuously to subjugate and oppress the peoples of those parts of the country which were more economically advanced than Serbia itself. It was largely as a result of this that peoples who had felt themselves one nation until the Republic of Yugoslavia was established after the first world war became sharply divided. In the atmosphere of acute national conflict which developed the people saw the monarchists, bankers, industrialists and landlords divide again, not on the basis of national interest but according to which group of the great powers each thought would emerge victorious. In contrast, the position of the

Communist Party proclaimed at Zagreb before the invasion and fought for after the occupation was always: "We are going to fight against the Italian fascists and the German Nazis to the last drop of our blood, but we are going to fight for the freedom of Yugoslavia, each of its nations, all of its people."

The old state apparatus broke down completely under the impact of invasion, desertion and military occupation by varied and changing armies. The people's war of liberation was, of necessity, waged against the administration of the invaders, therefore the partisans set up their own local People's Authorities in all liberated areas. Concerning these "National Liberation Committees," Marshal Tito writes: "That we had discerned the wishes of the people was apparent from the fact that the people immediately started setting up such committees, not only throughout the liberated territory but in all towns and villages situated in parts which had not been liberated."

The authorities were separate national organizations in Serbia, Croatia, Slovenia, etc. This corresponded with the needs and the exigencies of the liberation struggle during that period, it also corresponded with the national aspirations of the people.

A Decentralized State of United Nationalities

The state form of the new Yugoslavia was not first worked out in theory; like Topsy, it "just grew". In 1943 the principle of federation was agreed upon and the aim of distinctive national identity for each of the five nations united in a Yugoslav Federation was proclaimed. National parliaments were established in the liberated territory of each republic. The basis of popular government authority was the People☐s Committees. To quote Marshal Tito again: "They were the rudiments of the new state which was gradually coming into being in the process of the liberation struggle."

It is largely a codification of that form of government and division of authority which was shaped and tested in the fire of war that the new constitution proclaims in its first article:

"The Federative People's Republic of Yugoslavia consists of two houses--the Federal Council and the Council of Nationalities. Members of the Federal Council are elected by free equal and secret ballot in elections in which every citizen of Yugoslavia eighteen gears of age of over, without regard to nationality, race or religion, enjoys the right to vote. Any citizen over the age of 18 has the full right to offer himself or herself for election and to be elected to either house. Delegates to the Council of Nationalities are elected in the republics, autonomous provinces and regions.

The citizens of each republic elect 30 representatives to the Council of Nationalities, the autonomous provinces elect 20, and autonomous regions 10 members. Thus while the Federal Council represents the people in general, at the rate of one representative for every 50,000 inhabitants, the Council of nationalities represents the different republics without regard to numbers. Each house has equal rights. No person can be a member of both of them at the same time. They sit simultaneously but (except is special circumstances) separately. Any bill may be initiated in either house, no bill can become law unless and until it receives a majority vote in both of them.

The second article of the constitution names the six republics. Article 6 provides that "All authority in the Federative Republic of Yugoslavia derives from the people," exercised "through freely elected representative organs of state authority, the people's committees which, from local people's committees up to the assemblies of the people's republics and the People's Assembly of the Federative People's Republic of Yugoslavia, originated and developed during the struggle for national liberation..." Article 9 provides that "The sovereignty of the people's republics composing the Federative People"s Republic of Yugoslavia is limited only by the rights which by this Constitution are given to the Federative People's Republic of Yugoslavia." Article 13 provides that "national minorities" enjoy the right to and protection of their own cultural development and the free use of their own language." In connection with that provision I should mention the fact that the national minorities enjoy all the rights of citizenship. For example, the Hungarians not only enjoy the franchise, schools in which instruction is in the Hungarian language, including high schools, and newspapers; they also share in local administration: in the areas where they are concentrated they receive a proportion of the seats in administrative bodies corresponding with the proportion that the Hungarians constitute the electorate. They also elect representatives to parliament.

Thus the state and governmental system of the new Yugoslavia includes all the fundamental and most democratic principles of parliamentary government as it has evolved particularly in Britain and the United States, as well as the vast extensions of democracy which originated in the Soviet Union.

First, there is the extremely broad popular base of state power guaranteed by the fundamental constitutional law that the representatives to all People's Authorities from local communities up must be elected by secret ballot in direct elections in which every citizen, male and female, eighteen years of age or over has the right to vote and to stand as a candidate.

Second, there is the constitutional provision, characteristic of the United States, that both houses of the National Assembly are equal.

Third, there is the fact, characteristic of the de British system and one of its greatest contributions to the development of democratic government, that the Prime Minister and Government are directly responsible to and dependent upon the elected representatives if the people. Furthermore, whereas in Canada Mr Ilsey, speaking for the government, declares that the power of cabinet derives from the King and not from the people, in Yugoslavia the Constitution proclaims that: "all authority in the Federative People's Republic of Yugoslavia derives from the people and belongs to the people."

102

Fourth, there is the fact that in new Yugoslavia the greatest contributions made to the development of democratic government by the Soviet Union are also included. The Council of Nationalities with its equal rights plus the basic People's Authorities, the local people's committees, create a synthesis of the most advanced features of democratic government as it has been developed from Oliver Cromwell to Lenin. This combination of the highest form of democratic government and the overwhelming popular vote (96 per cent. cast in support of the aims of the present National Front government), is the revolutionary content of the new Yugoslav state.

Yugoslavia has dealt with both its economic and its national problem in a radical and audacious manner. It is demonstrating that in the conditions created by the people's war for freedom it is possible to carry through such policies without proletarian dictatorship. It is obvious that the people are united and solidly behind their government. Indeed, with such decentralization of authority, such wide functions and powers reserved for the governments of the national republics, the unity, or conversely the disunity if the people will determine everything. The very fact that there is now demonstrated such unity of purpose, enthusiastic support for the central government and such widespread and continuous sefl-sacrificing effort to achieve its aims is, in the conditions created by the new constitution, the clearest evidence that the people are behind the government which they elected to direct the efforts of all the people and all the country's resources to achievement of the aims proclaimed by the united national liberation movement.

There is the answer to the question: "What sort of state is the new Yugoslavia?" While it is not a soviet state, it is a new type of democratic people's state, with a fundamentally different structure and functions from those of a capitalist state, and representing an entirely different social basis than does any capitalist state. It is a people's republic in place of the old monarchy. It is a state founded upon and expressing a completely democratic and just solution of the national question. It is based upon the principles of the fullest people's democracy and the planned development of all the productive possibilities of the country for the welfare of all the people. Through this new people's state, in its totality of local People's Committees, National Republic governments and Federal government, the People's Authority combine to constitute a state form and content which will enable the people to abolish the exploitation of man by man--to build a socialist Yugoslavs.

Notes

1. The above quotations are excerpts only. For the full texts of the articles from which I have quoted see The Constitution of the Federative People's Republic of Yugoslavia.

2. The Specific Character of the Liberation Struggle and the Revolutionary Transformation of Yugoslavia--The Communist, organ of the Central Committee of the C.P. of Yugoslavia, October, 1946.

6. It isn't Over Yet

The people of Europe want peace. They want food and clothing also, and in many places their need is urgent and stark. But above all other of their string desires they want to be free: free to decide for themselves what sort of governments they are to have, who are to head their governments and what national aims their governments shall represent. They feel the more strongly on this point because of their bitter and tragic experiences during the past nine years. A hundred million or them see in the calculated United States and Canadian discrimination against the new democracies evidence of a cynical effort to re-establish the conditions which existed before the war. Against that the overwhelming majority of them are united solidly.

They want the sympathy and the help of the democratic people of Canada and the United States. A cabinet minister who was previously a school teacher said to me: "If only the people of North America realized that we are very similar people to themselves, trying to do exactly the sort of things that they would want to do if they were here in our conditions, I'm sure they would want to help us."

That is true. Every democratic man and women in Canada who understands the facts does want to help; not alone because it is the decent and democratic thing to do, but because the reconstruction of Europe is an indispensable need if we are to have a peaceful and prosperous postwar world. As Marshal Tito said to Bill Foster when the latter commented upon the Truman atomic bomb policy as a permanent threat of war: "It isn't the atomic bomb that worries the peoples of Europe today, but the need to restore our industries."

Democratic Canadians can help the peoples of Europe to restore their industries. All of them will need goods which

Canada exports. All of them will be able to pay for such goods if they are given assistance and time to restore their domestic production. Canada can afford to give credit to these countries. After the first world war Canada gave a credit of twenty-five million dollars to the reactionary monarchist government of Yugoslavia; how much more easily our government could afford to extend credit to the people's government of Yugoslavia today!

Immediately after the war the Dominion government did extend a small credit to Czechoslovakia (a total overall credit of nineteen million dollars). But the Canadian government has cancelled that credit since, and it is impossible to ignore the significance of the fact that it was cancelled shortly after the United States government cancelled the credit it had granted to Czechoslovakia before the people there elected a people's government headed by a communist.

Democratic Canadians welcomed the government's billion and a quarter loan to Britain and the generous terms upon which it was granted. They welcomed the loan of two hundred and forty-five million dollars to France, and the money loaned to the government of Holland to aid that country in its gigantic task of postwar reconstruction. But democratic Canadians could not approve of that large part of the loan to Holland which was earmarked for the specific purpose of helping Dutch finance-capitalist interests to crush the Indonesian People's Republic; especially when they realized that it was *given* for the same reasons that loans and credits to the new democracies or the soviet Union are *refused*. Against that use of the public treasury of Canada in the interest of finance-capitalist reaction every democratic Canadian should protest by all means at his or her command.

Whether or not Canada grants them credits the people of the U.S.S.R. and the people of Europe's new democracies are going to win. Democracy is on the march in the old world; it won't be stopped by economic discrimination, it won't be stopped bu lying propaganda, it won't be stopped even by the hunger suffered as a result of the Truman policy of using food as a weapon of political warfare. Just as the people of the Soviet Union met those same methods of discrimination during the 1920's and defeated them, so they and the people of the new democracies will defeat them now--and with the new democracies there are a hundred million mire of them now than there were in the 1920's.

Jacques Duclos summed it up when he said to Bill Foster and me: "The decisive question today is not 'is there or is there not a war danger?'. The decisive question for individuals, parties and governments is 'where do you stand?'. Two great bodies of opinion are competing for men's support. It is not true to say that this contest is between the Soviet Union and the United States, because it is going on in every corner of the civilized world. It is true, however, that the contest comes into the sharpest focus and is moire obvious between the struggle for the new democract of which the decisive centre is as yet in Europe and the struggle to re-stabilize imperialism, of which the decisive centre is now the United States. It is quite clear that the one means by which the danger of a third world war can be eliminated is by giving us in Europe sufficient time to show that the tremendous human advance achieved by the people of the U.S.S.R. on the ruins of Czarism can be surpassed by the people of Europe building on the ruins of Hitlerism."

That's all they are asking, time to build their new life in old Europe. Let's make Canada one of the countries from which they receive aid.

www.ingramcontent.com/pod-product-compliance
Lightning Source LLC
Chambersburg PA
CBHW070201290526
45789CB00002B/857